RANKING

THE

FIRST LADIES

RANKING

THE

FIRST LADIES

True Tales and Trivia, from
Martha Washington to Michelle Obama

IAN RANDAL STROCK

Carrel Books

Carrel Books books may be purchased in bulk at special discounts for sales promotion, corporate gifts, fund-raising, or educational purposes. Special editions can also be created to specifications. For details, contact the Special Sales Department, Carrel Books, 307 West 36th Street, 11th Floor, New York, NY 10018 or carrelbooks@skyhorsepublishing.com.

Carrel Books® is a registered trademark of Skyhorse Publishing, Inc.®, a Delaware corporation.

Visit our website at www.carrelbooks.com.
10 9 8 7 6 5 4 3 2 1

Library of Congress Cataloging-in-Publication Data is available on file.

Cover design by Rain Saukas

Print ISBN: 978-1-63144-058-8
Ebook ISBN: 978-1-63144-060-1

Printed in the United States of America

For Mom.

CONTENTS

INTRODUCTION

When I was little, my mother hung a poster in the house, showing the Presidents' faces, names, and dates of office. I memorized it.

Soon after that, President Nixon announced his resignation, and my first political memory is asking my parents if that meant that Henry Kissinger would be President, since his was the only other name I knew. My parents explained to me about the Vice Presidency and that Gerald Ford was the new President.

Then I learned more about the Presidents—who they were, what they did, how they came to be President—and I developed more and more of an interest in them. I began looking for commonalities, connections between the men who'd been President, patterns and signs. What characteristics did they share? What facets of their lives pointed toward their eventual elections? Could I calculate all the numbers to predict who would become the next President? Could I use the information I gathered to earn that post myself?

As it turns out, the answers are equivocal. Using those numbers, I was able to predict Barack Obama's election over John McCain and then his reelection over Mitt Romney. But I did not share those commonalities the Presidents seemed to have, so my odds of getting there are very long indeed.

While I was turning this lifelong interest in the Presidents into my first book (*The Presidential Book of Lists*, which Random House/Villard published before the election of 2008), I was also looking at those closest to them: spouses, children, parents, and more. And just as I was fascinated by

1

the Presidents, individually and collectively, their relatives proved to be no less interesting, especially their First Ladies. While they do not fit into the same patterns as easily as the Presidents, they are a varied, accomplished, and interesting lot.

Thus, I am pleased to present this book. Originally conceived as a companion to my first, it has grown into a stand-alone volume. I hope you'll enjoy learning more about the First Ladies, as I did in preparing this book.

The First Ladies

In the early days of the United States of America, the concept of a popularly elected President who would willingly step down from office after a set period of time was remarkable, nearly unprecedented. And when the government was set up, the President's spouse was not really considered, and there was no formal legislation surrounding her. Neither was there a generally accepted term. Though the President was called "the President" or "Mr. President," his wife would be known howsoever she requested. Martha Washington was usually called Lady Washington or Mrs. President, and sometimes the term "Presidentress" was used.

According to legend, President Zachary Taylor was the first to use the term "First Lady," when he was eulogizing former First Lady Dolley Madison in 1849. Unfortunately, no record of his eulogy exists.

President James Buchanan's niece, Harriet Lane, who was his official hostess, was the first woman to be called First Lady while actually serving in that position. The phrase appeared in print in Frank Leslie's *Illustrated Monthly* in 1860, when he wrote, "The Lady of the White House, and by courtesy, the First Lady of the Land." As late as the second decade of the 1900s, other terms were used, including Edith Wilson's preferred "Mrs. Presidentress."

Today, the title First Lady of the United States is recognized as the official White House hostess. The last time there was no Presidential wife to fulfill that role was 1914–15, after Ellen Wilson died and before Woodrow Wilson married Edith Galt. Since then, every President's wife has been active in the role, so it has come to be synonymous with the President's wife.

The position of the First Lady is not elected, and it has no official duties and no salary. Nevertheless, it has evolved into a post of significant influence. Most First Ladies champion charitable causes and serve as role models. The first First Ladies, Martha Washington and Abigail Adams, came to prominence during the Revolutionary War, and while their husbands were President, they were treated as if they were "ladies" of the British royal court, elevated supporters of the sovereign. Dolley Madison popularized the role and was cognizant of her position as a role model. She set a standard for many of her successors.

After more than a century of First Ladies confining themselves to the social and supportive aspects of life, Woodrow Wilson's second wife, Edith, broke out of those constraints and greatly (if secretly) expanded the role of First Lady. She is generally assumed to have been acting President for six months following his stroke in 1919. This position was not Constitutional: Vice President Marshall was kept from seeing the President or knowing the full extent of his incapacity. If Marshall had visited the ailing President, it is probable he would have moved to be acting President himself or possibly sought Wilson's removal from the Presidency. But history records that he did not, and Edith always claimed that Woodrow made all the decisions and signed all the papers, which she brought him in private.

It wasn't until Eleanor Roosevelt in the 1930s that the First Lady took on more executive responsibilities. Franklin was wheelchair-bound and thus unable to travel easily. Eleanor took on a lot of travel for her President-husband, performing inspections and meeting the people in places Franklin could not easily go, being seen in public, and coincidentally assuming a position of power herself. Eleanor also recognized her public persona, and in addition to the duties she carried out for the President, she wrote her own syndicated newspaper column and hosted a radio show. After Franklin's death, President Truman officially recognized her importance to the country by appointing her US Delegate to the United Nations.

Hillary Clinton was the first First Lady to have a formal job in her husband's Administration, managing its efforts to reform healthcare from her precedent-setting office in the West Wing of the White House.

The Office of the First Lady of the United States handles her hostessing, social, and ceremonial duties. The Office now has a paid staff and is part of the Executive Office of the President, but it wasn't always so.

Caroline Harrison's niece Mary Scott Lord Dimmick (who later married Caroline's widowed husband) may have been the first staff member for a First Lady. Mary served as Caroline's social secretary. Florence Harding had a "funded staff," including a social secretary and an assistant. Eleanor Roosevelt had a staff of only two. At first, they worked out of a second-floor office in the Executive Mansion, but later initiated the use of a First Lady's office in the newly constructed East Wing. Jacqueline Kennedy expanded the First Lady's staff to 40 people, directed by the social secretary. The current Office of the First Lady includes a Chief of Staff, Senior Advisor, Director of Communications, Press Secretary, Director of Strategic Planning, and Director of Special Projects, as well as assistants and more.

Rosalynn Carter sat in on Cabinet meetings, focused on substantive policy issues, and her husband cited her as an equal partner, calling her a "perfect extension of myself." In 1979, *Time* magazine called her the "second most powerful person in the United States." Under Rosalynn Carter, the office was, for the first time, formally called "Office of the First Lady." Her principal assistant, Mary Finch Hoyt, was the first to be called "Chief of Staff to the First Lady." A 1978 law finally authorized government funding for the First Lady's staff and office, though curiously, the First Lady herself is still an unfunded and undefined position.

Note on Usage

The term "First Lady" didn't come into widespread use until the late 1800s, and even into the early 1900s, its use was not universal. While it's generally used today to mean the President's wife, in point of fact, the government recognizes the term as referring to whoever serves as the "official White House hostess." In this book, however, I've slightly modified the definition for simplicity's sake: in these pages, "First Lady" means any woman who was married to a President before, during, or after his term of office. I've also back dated the usage to the beginning of the republic, so that Martha Washington is the first First Lady. And Martha Jefferson, though she died 18 years before her husband was elected President, was also a First Lady.

Several Presidents served without a living spouse or with a spouse who was unwilling to take on White House hostessing duties (such as Jane Pierce, whose melancholia kept her secluded for almost two years, or Ida McKinley, whose illness kept her from most hostessing duties, which instead fell to Second Lady Jennie Hobart). In those cases, there were usually official White House hostesses, but only one, James Buchanan's niece Harriet Lane, is usually included on the list of First Ladies. But because in this book First Ladies are the women who married Presidents, see Chapter 30 for a discussion of the other official White House hostesses.

In researching this book and its predecessor—*The Presidential Book of Lists: From Most to Least, Elected to Rejected, Worst to Cursed—Fascinating Facts About Our Chief Executives*, which focuses on the Presidents—I discovered that there are several methods of determining how closely two people are related. I've decided to use the method advocated by the National Genealogical Society, which seems the most common. In this system, to determine what degree of cousins two people are, count generations back to the common ancestor from each of the two people being compared. Using the person most closely related to the common ancestor, the degree of cousinhood (first, second, etc.) is one less than the number of generations between them. The degree of removedness (once removed, twice removed, etc.) is the number of generations difference between the two people being compared.

Common Ancestor	Child	Grandchild	Great-Grandchild	Great-Great-Grandchild	Great(3)-Grandchild
Child	Siblings	Nephew	Grand-Nephew	Great-Nephew	Great-Great-Nephew
Grandchild	Nephew	First Cousins	First Cousins, Once Removed	First Cousins, Twice Removed	First Cousins, Three Times Removed
Great-Grandchild	Grand-Nephew	First Cousins, Once Removed	Second Cousins	Second Cousins, Once Removed	Second Cousins, Twice Removed
Great-Great-Grandchild	Great-Nephew	First Cousins, Twice Removed	Second Cousins, Once Removed	Third Cousins	Third Cousins, Once Removed
Great(3)-Grandchild	Great-Great-Nephew	First Cousins, Three Times Removed	Second Cousins, Twice Removed	Third Cousins, Once Removed	Fourth Cousins

For example, James Madison and Zachary Taylor shared a pair of great-grandparents, Col. James Taylor and Martha Thompson. Their daughter Frances was President Madison's grandmother, while their son Zachary was President Taylor's grandfather. So we use the box on the left side for "great-grandchild" (James Madison) and the box at the top for "great-grandchild" (Zachary Taylor) and where those lines intersect, we see that they are second cousins. If, for another example, the common ancestors had been Zachary Taylor's great-great-grandparents, we would use that line on the top to find that the two Presidents were second cousins, once removed.

When discussing grandparents and grandchildren, I've used a parenthetical number for more than two greats, for simplicity's sake. Thus, great(5)-grandparents means great-great-great-great-great-grandparents.

The information in this book is current as of December 31, 2015. For the latest news and updates, read my blog at uspresidents.livejournal.com or IanRandalStrock.com.

General Information about the Presidents

Name	Birth Date	Birthplace	Presidency	Death Date	Burial Place	Party	Vice President
George Washington	February 22, 1732	Westmoreland County, VA	April 30, 1789– March 4, 1797	December 14, 1799	Mt. Vernon, VA	Fed	John Adams
John Adams	October 30, 1735	Quincy, MA	March 4, 1797– March 4, 1801	July 4, 1826	Quincy, MA	Fed	Thomas Jefferson
Thomas Jefferson	April 13, 1743	Albemarle County, VA	March 4, 1801– March 4, 1809	July 4, 1826	Monticello estate, Charlottesville, VA	Dem-Rep	Aaron Burr / George Clinton
James Madison	March 16, 1751	King George County, VA	March 4, 1809– March 4, 1817	June 28, 1836	Montpelier estate, VA	Dem-Rep	George Clinton / Elbridge Gerry
James Monroe	April 28, 1758	Westmoreland County, VA	March 4, 1817– March 4, 1825	July 4, 1831	New York, NY (1831–58), Richmond, VA	Dem-Rep	Daniel D. Tompkins
John Quincy Adams	July 11, 1767	Quincy, MA	March 4, 1825– March 4, 1829	February 23, 1848	Quincy, MA	Dem-Rep	John C. Calhoun
Andrew Jackson	March 15, 1767	Waxhaws, SC	March 4, 1829– March 4, 1837	June 8, 1845	Hermitage estate, Nashville, TN	Dem	John C. Calhoun /Martin Van Buren
Martin Van Buren	December 5, 1782	Kinderhook, NY	March 4, 1837– March 4, 1841	July 24, 1862	Kinderhook, NY	Dem	Richard M. Johnson

Name	Birth Date	Birthplace	Presidency	Death Date	Burial Place	Party	Vice President
William Henry Harrison	February 9, 1773	Charles City County, VA	March 4, 1841–April 4, 1841	April 4, 1841	North Bend, OH	Whig	John Tyler
John Tyler	March 29, 1790	Charles City County, VA	April 6, 1841–March 4, 1845	January 18, 1862	Richmond, VA	Whig	
James Knox Polk	November 2, 1795	Mecklenburg County, NC	March 4, 1845–March 4, 1849	June 15, 1849	Polk Place, TN (1849–1893), Nashville, TN	Dem	George M. Dallas
Zachary Taylor	November 24, 1784	Orange County, VA	March 4, 1849–July 9, 1850	July 9, 1850	Louisville, KY	Whig	Millard Fillmore
Millard Fillmore	January 7, 1800	Locke Township, NY	July 10, 1850–March 4, 1853	March 8, 1874	Buffalo, NY	Whig	
Franklin Pierce	November 23, 1804	Hillsborough, NH	March 4, 1853–March 4, 1857	October 8, 1869	Concord, NH	Dem	William R. King
James Buchanan	April 23, 1791	near Cove Gap, PA	March 4, 1857–March 4, 1861	June 1, 1868	Lancaster, PA	Dem	John C. Breckinridge
Abraham Lincoln	February 12, 1809	near Hodgenville, KY	March 4, 1861–April 15, 1865	April 15, 1865	Springfield, IL	Rep	Hannibal Hamlin/Andrew Johnson
Andrew Johnson	December 29, 1808	Raleigh, NC	April 15, 1865–March 4, 1869	July 31, 1875	Greeneville, TN	National Union	

Name	Birth Date	Birthplace	Presidency	Death Date	Burial Place	Party	Vice President
Ulysses Simpson Grant	April 27, 1822	Port Pleasant, OH	March 4, 1869– March 4, 1877	July 23, 1885	New York, NY	Rep	Schuyler Colfax/ Henry Wilson
Rutherford Birchard Hayes	October 4, 1822	Delaware, OH	March 4, 1877– March 4, 1881	January 17, 1893	Oakwood Cemetery, Fremont, OH (1893–1915), Spiegel Grove, Fremont, OH	Rep	William A. Wheeler
James Abram Garfield	November 19, 1831	Orange, OH	March 4, 1881– September 19, 1881	September 19, 1881	Cleveland, OH	Rep	Chester Alan Arthur
Chester Alan Arthur	October 5, 1830	North Fairfield, VT	September 20, 1881–March 4, 1885	November 18, 1886	Albany, NY	Rep	
Grover Cleveland	March 18, 1837	Caldwell, NJ	March 4, 1885– March 4, 1889; March 4, 1893– March 4, 1897	June 24, 1908	Princeton, NJ	Dem	Thomas A. Hendricks / Adlai E. Stevenson
Benjamin Harrison	August 20, 1833	North Bend, OH	March 4, 1889– March 4, 1893	March 13, 1901	Indianapolis, IN	Rep	Levi P. Morton

Name	Birth Date	Birthplace	Presidency	Death Date	Burial Place	Party	Vice President
William McKinley	January 29, 1843	Niles, OH	March 4, 1897–September 14, 1901	September 14, 1901	Westlawn Cemetery, Canton, OH (1901–1907), McKinley National Memorial, Canton, OH	Rep	Garret A. Hobart/Theodore Roosevelt
Theodore Roosevelt	October 27, 1858	New York, NY	September 14, 1901–March 4, 1909	January 6, 1919	Oyster Bay, NY	Rep	Charles W. Fairbanks
William Howard Taft	September 15, 1857	Cincinnati, OH	March 4, 1909–March 4, 1913	March 8, 1930	Arlington National Cemetery, VA	Rep	James S. Sherman
Woodrow Wilson	December 28, 1856	Staunton, VA	March 4, 1913–March 4, 1921	February 3, 1924	Washington Cathedral, Washington, DC	Dem	Thomas R. Marshall
Warren Gamaliel Harding	November 2, 1865	Corsica, OH	March 4, 1921–August 2, 1923	August 2, 1923	Marion, OH	Rep	Calvin Coolidge
Calvin Coolidge	July 4, 1872	Plymouth, VT	August 3, 1923–March 4, 1929	January 5, 1933	Plymouth, VT	Rep	Charles G. Dawes

Name	Birth Date	Birthplace	Presidency	Death Date	Burial Place	Party	Vice President
Herbert Clark Hoover	August 10, 1874	West Branch, IA	March 4, 1929–March 4, 1933	October 20, 1964	West Branch, IA	Rep	Charles Curtis
Franklin Delano Roosevelt	January 30, 1882	Hyde Park, NY	March 4, 1933–April 12, 1945	April 12, 1945	Hyde Park, NY	Dem	John Nance Garner/Henry Agard Wallace/ Harry S Truman
Harry S Truman	May 8, 1884	Lamar, MO	April 12, 1945–January 20, 1953	December 26, 1972	Truman Library, Independence, MO	Dem	Alben W. Barkley
Dwight David Eisenhower	October 14, 1890	Denison, TX	January 20, 1953–January 20, 1961	March 28, 1969	Abilene, KS	Rep	Richard Milhous Nixon
John Fitzgerald Kennedy	May 29, 1917	Brookline, MA	January 20, 1961–November 22, 1963	November 22, 1963	Arlington National Cemetery, VA	Dem	Lyndon Baines Johnson
Lyndon Baines Johnson	August 27, 1908	near Johnson City, TX	November 22, 1963–January 20, 1969	January 22, 1973	LBJ Ranch, Johnson City, TX	Dem	Hubert H. Humphrey
Richard Milhous Nixon	January 9, 1913	Yorba Linda, CA	January 20, 1969–August 9, 1974	April 22, 1994	Nixon Library and Museum, Yorba Linda, CA	Rep	Spiro T. Agnew/ Gerald Rudolph Ford

Name	Birth Date	Birthplace	Presidency	Death Date	Burial Place	Party	Vice President
Gerald Rudolph Ford	July 14, 1913	Omaha, NE	August 9, 1974–January 20, 1977	December 26, 2006	Ford Library and Museum, Grand Rapids, MI	Rep	Nelson A. Rockefeller
James Earl "Jimmy" Carter	October 1, 1924	Plains, GA	January 20, 1977–January 20, 1981			Dem	Walter Mondale
Ronald Wilson Reagan	February 6, 1911	Tampico, IL	January 20, 1981–January 20, 1989	June 5, 2004	Reagan Library, Simi Valley, CA	Rep	George H.W. Bush
George H.W. Bush	June 12, 1924	Milton, MA	January 20, 1989–January 20, 1993			Rep	J. Danforth Quayle
William Jefferson Clinton	August 19, 1946	Hope, AR	January 20, 1993–January 20, 2001			Dem	Al Gore, Jr.
George W. Bush	July 6, 1946	New Haven, CT	January 20, 2001–January 20, 2009			Rep	Richard Bruce Cheney
Barack H. Obama	August 4, 1961	Honolulu, HI	January 20, 2009–			Dem	Joe Biden

General Information about the First Ladies

Name	Birth Date	Birthplace	Marriage Date	Term as First Lady	Death Date	Burial Place
Martha Dandridge Custis Washington	June 2, 1731	New Kent County, VA	January 6, 1759	April 30, 1789– March 4, 1797	May 22, 1802	Mount Vernon, VA
Abigail Smith Adams	November 11, 1744	Weymouth, MA	October 25, 1764	March 4, 1797– March 4, 1801	October 28, 1818	Quincy, MA
Martha Wayles Skelton Jefferson	October 30, 1748	Charles City County, VA	January 1, 1772		September 6, 1782	Monticello, VA
Dolley Payne Todd Madison	May 20, 1768	New Garden, NC	September 15, 1794	March 4, 1809– March 4, 1817	July 12, 1849	Washington, DC, then Montpelier, VA
Elizabeth Kortright Monroe	June 30, 1768	New York, NY	February 16, 1786	March 4, 1817– March 4, 1825	September 23, 1830	Richmond, VA
Louisa Catherine Johnson Adams	February 12, 1775	London, England	July 26, 1797	March 4, 1825– March 4, 1829	May 15, 1852	Quincy, MA

Name	Birth Date	Birthplace	Marriage Date	Term as First Lady	Death Date	Burial Place
Rachel Donelson Robards Jackson	June 15, 1767	Halifax County, VA	August 1791/ January 17, 1794		December 22, 1828	Hermitage estate, Nashville, TN
Hannah Hoes Van Buren	March 8, 1783	Kinderhook, NY	February 21, 1807		February 5, 1819	Kinderhook, NY
Anna Tuthill Symmes Harrison	July 25, 1775	Morristown, NJ	November 25, 1795	March 4, 1841– April 4, 1841	February 25, 1864	North Bend, OH
Letitia Christian Tyler	November 12, 1790	Cedar Grove plantation, New Kent County, VA	March 29, 1813	April 4, 1841– September 10, 1842	September 10, 1842	Cedar Grove plantation, New Kent County, VA
Julia Gardiner Tyler	July 23, 1820 (Family records are not certain regarding the exact day of her birth in 1820. Some indicate it was May 4. Her grave stone says July 23.)	Long Island, NY	June 26, 1844	June 26, 1844– March 4, 1845	July 10, 1889	Richmond, VA

Name	Birth Date	Birthplace	Marriage Date	Term as First Lady	Death Date	Burial Place
Sarah Childress Polk	September 4, 1803	Murfreesboro, TN	January 1, 1824	March 4, 1845–March 4, 1849	August 14, 1891	Nashville, TN
Margaret "Peggy" Mackall Smith Taylor	September 21, 1788	Calvert County, MD	June 21, 1810	March 4, 1849–July 9, 1850	August 14, 1852	Louisville, KY
Abigail Powers Fillmore	March 13, 1798	Stillwater, NY	February 5, 1826	July 9, 1850–March 4, 1853	March 30, 1853	Buffalo, NY
Caroline Carmichael McIntosh Fillmore	October 21, 1813	Morristown, NJ	February 10, 1858		August 11, 1881	Buffalo, NY
Jane Means Appleton Pierce	March 12, 1806	Hampton, NH	November 19, 1834	March 4, 1853–March 4, 1857	December 2, 1863	Concord, NH
Mary Todd Lincoln	December 13, 1818	Lexington, KY	November 4, 1842	March 4, 1861–April 15, 1865	July 16, 1882	Springfield, IL
Eliza McCardle Johnson	October 4, 1810	Leesburg, TN	May 17, 1827	April 15, 1865–March 4, 1869	January 15, 1876	Greeneville, TN
Julia Boggs Dent Grant	January 26, 1826	St. Louis, MO	August 22, 1848	March 4, 1869–March 4, 1877	December 14, 1902	New York, NY

Name	Birth Date	Birthplace	Marriage Date	Term as First Lady	Death Date	Burial Place
Lucy Ware Webb Hayes	August 28, 1831	Chillicothe, OH	December 30, 1852	March 4, 1877– March 4, 1881	June 25, 1889	Spiegel Grove, Fremont, OH
Lucretia "Crete" Rudolph Garfield	April 19, 1832	Hiram, OH	November 11, 1858	March 4, 1881– September 19, 1881	March 14, 1918	Cleveland, OH
Ellen "Nell" Lewis Herndon Arthur	August 30, 1837	Culpepper Court House, VA	October 25, 1859		January 12, 1880	Albany, NY
Frances Folsom Cleveland	July 21, 1864	Buffalo, NY	June 2, 1886	June 2, 1886– March 4, 1889; March 4, 1893– March 4, 1897	October 29, 1947	Princeton, NJ
Caroline Lavinia Scott Harrison	October 1, 1832	Oxford, OH	October 20, 1853	March 4, 1889– October 25, 1892	October 25, 1892	Indianapolis, IN
Mary Scott Lord Dimmick Harrison	April 30, 1858	Honesdale, PA	April 6, 1896		January 5, 1948	Indianapolis, IN
Ida Saxton McKinley	June 8, 1847	Canton, OH	January 25, 1871	March 4, 1897– September 14, 1901	May 26, 1907	Canton, OH

Name	Birth Date	Birthplace	Marriage Date	Term as First Lady	Death Date	Burial Place
Alice Hathaway Lee Roosevelt	July 29, 1861	Chestnut Hill, MA	October 27, 1880		February 14, 1884	Cambridge, MA
Edith Kermit Carow Roosevelt	August 6, 1861	Norwich, CT	December 2, 1886	September 14, 1901–March 4, 1909	September 30, 1948	Oyster Bay, NY
Helen "Nellie" Herron Taft	June 2, 1861	Cincinnati, OH	June 19, 1886	March 4, 1909–March 4, 1913	May 22, 1943	Arlington National Cemetery, VA
Ellen Louise Axson Wilson	May 15, 1860	Savannah, GA	June 24, 1885	March 4, 1913–August 6, 1914	August 6, 1914	Rome, GA
Edith Bolling Galt Wilson	October 15, 1872	Wytheville, VA	December 18, 1915	December 18, 1915–March 4, 1921	December 28, 1961	National Cathedral, Washington, DC
Florence "Flossie" Mabel Kling DeWolfe Harding	August 15, 1860	Marion, OH	July 8, 1891	March 4, 1921–August 3, 1923	November 21, 1924	Marion, OH
Grace Anna Goodhue Coolidge	January 3, 1879	Burlington, VT	October 4, 1905	August 3, 1923–March 4, 1929	July 8, 1957	Plymouth, VT

Name	Birth Date	Birthplace	Marriage Date	Term as First Lady	Death Date	Burial Place
Lou Henry Hoover	March 29, 1874	Waterloo, IA	February 10, 1899	March 4, 1929– March 4, 1933	January 7, 1944	Palo Alto, CA / West Branch, IA
Anna Eleanor Roosevelt Roosevelt	October 11, 1884	New York, NY	March 17, 1905	March 4, 1933– April 12, 1945	November 7, 1962	Hyde Park, NY
Elizabeth "Bess" Virginia Wallace Truman	February 13, 1885	Independence, MO	June 28, 1919	April 12, 1945– January 20, 1953	October 18, 1982	Truman Library, Independence, MO
Marie "Mamie" Geneva Doud Eisenhower	November 14, 1896	Boone, IA	July 1, 1916	January 20, 1953–January 20, 1961	November 1, 1979	Abilene, KS
Jacqueline Lee Bouvier Kennedy Onassis	July 28, 1929	Southampton, NY	September 12, 1953	January 20, 1961– November 22, 1963	May 19, 1994	Arlington National Cemetery, VA
Claudia Alta "Lady Bird" Taylor Johnson	December 22, 1912	Karnack, TX	November 17, 1934	November 22, 1963–January 20, 1969	July 11, 2007	LBJ Ranch, Johnson Cty, TX

Name	Birth Date	Birthplace	Marriage Date	Term as First Lady	Death Date	Burial Place
Thelma Catherine "Patricia" "Pat" Ryan Nixon	March 16, 1912	Ely, NV	June 21, 1940	January 20, 1969–August 9, 1974	June 22, 1993	Nixon Library and Museum, Yorba Linda, CA
Elizabeth Ann "Betty" Bloomer Warren Ford	April 8, 1918	Chicago, IL	October 15, 1948	August 9, 1974–January 20, 1977	July 8, 2011	Ford Library and Museum, Grand Rapids, MI
Eleanor Rosalynn Smith Carter	August 18, 1927	Plains, GA	July 7, 1946	January 20, 1977–January 20, 1981		
Sarah Jane Faulks, aka Jane Wyman Reagan	January 5, 1917 (claimed January 4, 1914)	St. Joseph, MO	January 26, 1940 (divorced in 1949)		September 10, 2007	Cathedral City, CA
Anne Frances Robbins, aka Nancy Davis Reagan	July 6, 1921	New York, NY	March 4, 1952	January 20, 1981–January 20, 1989		
Barbara Pierce Bush	June 8, 1925	Rye, NY	January 6, 1945	January 20, 1989–January 20, 1993		

Name	Birth Date	Birthplace	Marriage Date	Term as First Lady	Death Date	Burial Place
Hillary Diane Rodham Clinton	October 26, 1947	Chicago, IL	October 11, 1975	January 20, 1993–January 20, 2001		
Laura Lane Welch Bush	November 4, 1946	Midland, TX	November 5, 1977	January 20, 2001–January 20, 2009		
Michelle LaVaughn Robinson Obama	January 17, 1964	Chicago, IL	October 3, 1992	January 20, 2009–		

THE AVERAGE FIRST LADY

Averages tell us about groups and enable us to make predictions about any member of the group, but they can't tell us about the possibility for something new. After gathering all the data, preparing this book, and calculating all the comparisons, I was also able to define the "Average First Lady." As with my Presidential book, this was one of my original goals, to figure out what qualities they all shared and see if those numbers might match myself (they don't). Additionally, to come up with these averages, some First Ladies have not been used (for instance, when calculating life span, the currently living First Ladies were not included). With those caveats, we can calculate the characteristics of an average Presidential spouse. She:

has a life expectancy of 69 years, 295 days (Lou Hoover is the most average in this respect, having lived 69 years, 284 days)

has a 42 percent chance of sharing her first name with another First Lady

has a one-in-three chance of having been born in New York or Virginia

has a better than one-in-three chance of being buried in Virginia or New York

has a 15 percent chance of dying on the same day (but not necessarily in the same year) as another First Lady has a 2 percent chance of having no living predecessors

has a 27 percent chance of being born in the same year as another First Lady

has a 20 percent chance of dying in the same year as another First Lady

has 3.4 children (2.0 sons, 1.4 daughters)

is 5 years, 316 days younger than her President-husband (Martha Jefferson is the most average in this respect; she was 5 years, 200 days younger than Thomas)

has 1.3 husbands

will die 5 years, 183 days after her President-husband (Ida McKinley is the most average in this respect; she died 5 years, 254 days after William)

has a 12.5 percent chance that her father will be alive to see her become First Lady

has a 28 percent chance that her mother will be alive to see her become First Lady

has a 63 percent chance of being an orphan when she becomes First Lady

has a 23 percent chance of being the firstborn child in her family

has a 13 percent chance of being the lastborn child in her family

has a 10 percent chance of being an only child

has a 23 percent chance that her father was some sort of farmer, planter, or landowner has a 19 percent chance that her father was some sort of merchant

has a 27 percent chance of being a college graduate

is 40 years, 104 days old when she becomes First Lady (Edith Roosevelt is the most average in this respect; she was 40 years, 39 days old when Theodore Roosevelt took the oath of office)

has a one-in-five chance of serving two full terms

will be First Lady for 4 years, 214 days (Ida McKinley is the most average in this respect; she was First Lady for 4 years, 194 days)

has a 30 percent chance of not being First Lady for the entire length of her husband's term of office.

THE FIRST LADIES: LIFE AND DEATH

1. The Five First Ladies Who Lived the Longest

1. ELIZABETH "BESS" TRUMAN (1945–53). Born on February 13, 1885, she was less than one year younger than her husband. She was 60 when she became First Lady and moved out of the White House nearly 30 years before she died, on October 18, 1982, aged 97 years, 247 days.

2. CLAUDIA "LADY BIRD" JOHNSON (1963–69). Born on December 22, 1912, she was 94 years, 201 days old when she died on July 11, 2007. She'd been a widow for more than 34 years.

3. NANCY REAGAN (1981–89) was born on July 6, 1921. She passed Betty Ford on October 5, 2014, and passed Lady Bird Johnson on January 23, 2016. Her husband, Ronald Reagan, was the second longest-lived President: he died at the age of 93 years, 121 days on June 5, 2004.

4. ELIZABETH "BETTY" FORD (1974–77). Born on April 8, 1918, she was 93 years, 91 days old when she died on July 8, 2011. Her husband, Gerald Ford, was the longest-lived President. He died at the age of 93 years, 164 days on December 26, 2006.

5. BARBARA BUSH (1989–93) is almost four years younger than Nancy Reagan. Born June 8, 1925, she passed Mary Harrison on August 21, 2014, and will pass Betty Ford on September 7, 2018.

The next two on the list are:

6. MARY HARRISON. The second wife of President Benjamin Harrison (1889–93), she married the former President in 1896. Mary was the niece of Benjamin's first wife, Caroline, who died in 1892 and was 25 years younger than her husband. She was born on April 30, 1858, and died on January 5, 1948, aged 89 years, 74 days.

7. ROSALYNN CARTER (1977–81) is two years younger than Barbara Bush. Born August 18, 1927, she'll pass Mary Harrison on November 1, 2016.

Ronald Reagan's first wife, JANE WYMAN (to whom he was married for a few years in the 1940s), was born on January 5, 1917 (though she claimed January 4, 1914) and died on September 10, 2007. Thus, if we count her as a First Lady, she would appear as #6 on this list, having lived 90 years, 248 days.

2. The Five First Ladies Who Died the Youngest

1. LETITIA TYLER (1841–42). Born on November 19, 1790, she was the first First Lady whose husband succeeded to the Presidency upon the death of his predecessor. She suffered a paralytic stroke in 1839, which left her an invalid. John Tyler became President on April 4, 1841, when Letitia was 50 years old. She suffered a second stroke and died of it on September 10, 1842, aged 51 years, 302 days. (He remarried two years later, the first President to marry while in office.)

2. ELLEN WILSON (1913–14). Born on May 15, 1860, she died of Bright's disease during her husband's first term of office, on August 6, 1914, aged 54 years, 83 days. (He remarried in December 1915.)

3. ABIGAIL FILLMORE (1850–53). Born on March 13, 1798, she is the first on this list to see her husband retire from the Presidency. She caught a cold at the inaugural festivities for her husband's successor, Franklin Pierce. The cold turned into pneumonia, and she died on March 30, 1853—26 days after Millard left office—at the age of 55 years, 17 days. (He remarried five years later.)

4. JANE PIERCE (1853–57). Born on March 12, 1806, she died of tuberculosis on December 2, 1863, aged 57 years, 265 days. Her husband outlived her by 12 years.

5. LUCY HAYES (1877–81). Born August 28, 1831, she lived 57 years, 301 days, dying of a stroke on June 25, 1889 (three and a half years before her husband).

The next two on the list (if we factor out those who died in office) are:

6. IDA MCKINLEY (1897–1901), who was born on June 8, 1847, and, widowed by William's assassination, died on May 26, 1907, aged 59 years, 352 days. She is the only one on this list to outlive her husband.

7. ELIZABETH MONROE (1817–25), who was born on June 30, 1768, and died on September 23, 1830, aged 62 years, 85 days.

In addition to the above list, there are also those wives who didn't live long enough to see their husbands become President:

1. ALICE ROOSEVELT. Theodore Roosevelt's first wife was born on July 29, 1861. They married on October 27, 1880, and then Alice died on February 14, 1884, aged 22 years, 200 days. Her death was due to Bright's disease and complications from childbirth (her daughter, Alice, who was named for her, was born on February 12, 1884). She died on the same day, and in the same house, as Theodore's mother.

2. MARTHA JEFFERSON. Thomas Jefferson's only wife was a widow when she married him. She was born on October 30, 1748, and they married on January 1, 1772. Martha died on September 6, 1782—four months after giving birth to her sixth child (only two lived to adulthood)—aged 33 years, 311 days. Jefferson became the third President in 1801, more than 18 years after her death.

3. HANNAH VAN BUREN. Born on March 8, 1783, she married Martin on February 21, 1807. She died of tuberculosis on February 5, 1819, aged 35 years, 334 days. Martin was elected Vice President in 1832 and President in 1836, taking office 18 years and one month after Hannah's death.

4. ELLEN "NELL" ARTHUR. Born on August 30, 1837, she married Chester on October 25, 1859. She died suddenly of pneumonia on January 12, 1880, aged 42 years 135 days. Chester was elected Vice President at the end of that year and succeeded to the Presidency in September 1881, following James Garfield's death in office.

5. RACHEL JACKSON. Born June 15, 1767, she married Lewis Robards in 1784, but it wasn't a happy marriage. He was a jealous man and sent her back to her parents, suing for divorce in 1790. Andrew mistakenly assumed that meant she was divorced, and Rachel and Andrew married in August 1791. When Robards learned of this "marriage," he sued for divorce on grounds of adultery, and the divorce was issued in September 1793. Rachel and Andrew remarried, or finally married, on January 17, 1794. She died suddenly on December 22, 1828, weeks after Andrew won the election, of illness brought on by the stress of the campaign. She was 61 years, 190 days old.

3. The First Ladies Who Lived the Longest after Leaving the White House

1. FRANCES CLEVELAND. Born July 21, 1864, she married President Grover Cleveland on June 2, 1886, becoming the youngest First Lady ever. Cleveland lost the election of 1888, but won the election of 1892. They retired from office for the final time on March 4, 1897. He died in 1908, and several years later, Frances became the first Presidential widow to remarry. By the time of her death, on October 29, 1947, she had been a retired First Lady for 50 years, 239 days.

2. JULIA TYLER. Born July 23, 1820, she married the recently widowed President John Tyler on June 26, 1844. They left office on March 4, 1845, and then had seven children together, before he died in 1862. She survived him by another 27 years. When she died, on July 10, 1889, she had been a retired First Lady for 44 years, 128 days.

3. SARAH POLK. Born September 4, 1803, she married James Knox Polk on January 1, 1824. He was President for one term, from March 4, 1845, to March 4, 1849, and died three months after leaving office. Sarah, however, survived much longer. She died on August 14, 1891, having been a retired First Lady for 42 years, 163 days, and a widow nearly all that time.

4. EDITH WILSON. Born October 15, 1872, she married the recently widowed President Woodrow Wilson on December 18, 1915. They left office on March 4, 1921. He died two and a half years later, but she survived and was prominent in the Washington, DC, social scene. She died on December 28, 1961, a retired First Lady for 40 years, 299 days.

5. EDITH ROOSEVELT. Born August 6, 1861, she married Theodore Roosevelt on December 2, 1886 (two years after his first wife's death). They had five children, and he became the youngest President ever when William McKinley died in office in 1901. Keeping a campaign promise to not seek another term, Theodore (and Edith) retired from office on March 4, 1909. He tried to make a comeback in 1912, but succeeded only in splitting his party and handing the election to Woodrow Wilson. He died in 1919, but Edith survived until September 30, 1948. At the time of her death, she had been a retired First Lady for 39 years, 210 days.

Five other First Ladies were retired for at least 30 years (only two Presidents have been retired more than 30 years: Herbert Hoover was retired for 31 years, 230 days; Jimmy Carter left office on January 20, 1981, and has been retired nearly 35 years at the time of this writing):

LADY BIRD JOHNSON: born December 22, 1912, she was First Lady from November 22, 1963, to January 20, 1969, and died July 11, 2007, having been retired for 38 years, 172 days.

LUCRETIA GARFIELD: born April 19, 1832, she was First Lady from March 4 to September 19, 1881, and died March 14, 1918, having been retired (and a widow) for 36 years, 176 days.

ROSALYNN CARTER: born August 18, 1927, she was First Lady from January 20, 1977, to January 20, 1981. At the time of this writing, she's been retired more than 34 years. She'll pass Edith Roosevelt for fifth place on this list on August 17, 2020 (one day before her 93rd birthday). She'll have to live to 104 to beat Frances Cleveland's record.

BETTY FORD: born April 8, 1918, she was First Lady from August 9, 1974, to January 20, 1977, and died July 8, 2011, having been retired for 34 years, 189 days.

DOLLEY MADISON: born May 20, 1768, she was First Lady from March 4, 1809, to March 4, 1817, and died July 12, 1849, having been retired for 32 years, 130 days.

JACQUELINE KENNEDY: born July 28, 1929, she was First Lady from January 20, 1961, to November 22, 1963, and died May 19, 1994, having been retired for 30 years, 178 days.

HELEN TAFT: born June 2, 1861, she was First Lady from March 4, 1909, to March 4, 1913, and died May 22, 1943, having been retired for 30 years, 79 days.

4. *The First Ladies Who Died the Soonest after Leaving the White House*

1. ABIGAIL FILLMORE. Born March 13, 1798, she married Millard Fillmore on February 5, 1826. She became First Lady when Zachary Taylor died in office on July 9, 1850. At the inaugural celebrations for Fillmore's successor, Franklin Pierce, on March 4, 1853, she caught a cold, which turned into pneumonia, and she died on March 30, 1853, having been retired for 26 days.

2. FLORENCE HARDING. Born August 15, 1860, she was a divorcée when she married Warren Harding, who was five years her junior, on July 8, 1891. She was First Lady from March 4, 1921, until he died in office on August 3, 1923. She was suffering from kidney disease when she died, on November 21, 1924. She had been a retired First Lady for only one year, 110 days.

3. MARGARET TAYLOR. Born September 21, 1788, she married Army Lieutenant Zachary Taylor on June 21, 1810 (he would later work his way up to general). He was elected President in 1848, and she was First Lady from March 4, 1849, until his death in office on July 9, 1850. Her health deteriorated quickly, and she died on August 14, 1852, having been a retired First Lady for two years, 36 days.

4. MARTHA WASHINGTON. Born June 2, 1731 (eight months before her future husband), she was a widow when she married George Washington on January 6, 1759. When he was the first President, from April 30, 1789, to March 4, 1797, the national capital was in New York City, and the term "First Lady" had not been invented. Nevertheless, when she died on May 22, 1802, she had been retired from the post of President's wife for five years, 79 days.

5. ELIZABETH MONROE. Born June 30, 1768, she was the first First Lady to be born in New York. She married James Monroe on February 16, 1786, and was First Lady from March 4, 1817, to March 4, 1825. She was chronically unwell and was severely burned while suffering a seizure in 1826. She died on September 23, 1830, having been retired for five years, 203 days.

6. IDA MCKINLEY. Born June 8, 1847, she was First Lady from March 4, 1897, until her husband's death in office on September 14, 1901. She died on May 26, 1907, after being a retired widow for five years, 254 days.

5. The Most Common Names
of First Ladies

Unlike their President-husbands, the First Ladies (and the wives of Presidents who didn't actually serve as First Lady) have far more unique names. Of the 48 Presidential spouses, there are 10 shared first names, and 31 that were unique. (Seven names account for 24 of the 43 men who were President.)

The 10 shared names are:

1. MARTHA. Martha Dandridge Custis Washington was the first First Lady, from 1789 to 1797. Martha Wayles Skelton Jefferson was the wife of third President Thomas Jefferson, though she died in 1782, 18 years before he was elected President.

2. ABIGAIL. Abigail Smith Adams was the wife of the first Vice President, John Adams, who became the second President (1797–1801). Abigail Powers Fillmore was the first wife of Millard Fillmore (1850–53), who died less than a month after he left office.

3. SARAH. Sarah Childress Polk was the wife of James Knox Polk, the youngest President to die after leaving office (he died at the age of 53). She outlived him by more than 46 years. Ronald Reagan's first wife, Jane Wyman, was born Sarah Jane Faulks but changed her name when she became an actress. They were married from 1940 to 1949; he was President from 1981 to 1989.

4. CAROLINE. Millard Fillmore's second wife, Caroline Carmichael McIntosh, married him five years after he retired from the Presidency. Benjamin Harrison's first wife, Caroline Lavinia Scott Harrison, died two weeks before he lost his bid for reelection in 1892.

5. JANE. Jane Means Appleton Pierce married Franklin Pierce in 1834, 18 years before he was elected President. Ronald Reagan's first wife (from 1940 to 1949) was the actress Jane Wyman (see "Sarah," above).

6. MARY. Mary Todd Lincoln was widowed when Abraham Lincoln became the first President to be assassinated, in April 1865. Mary Scott Lord Dimmick Harrison was Benjamin Harrison's first wife's niece and younger than his grown children when he married her after retiring from the Presidency.

7. ELLEN. Ellen Lewis Herndon Arthur died in January 1880. Her husband, Chester, was elected Vice President that November and then became President when James Garfield succumbed to gunshot wounds in September 1881. Ellen Louise Axson Wilson died midway through her husband Woodrow Wilson's first term, in 1914.

8. EDITH. Edith Kermit Carow Roosevelt was Theodore Roosevelt's second wife and his First Lady. She outlived both her husband and his cousin, President Franklin Roosevelt, and died in 1948. Edith Bolling Galt Wilson was introduced to President Woodrow Wilson less than a year after his first wife (see "Ellen," above) had died. She married him in 1915.

9. ELEANOR. Eleanor Roosevelt's given name was Anna, but she never used it. And when she married her distant cousin Franklin in 1905, she didn't have to change her last name (her uncle, President Theodore Roosevelt, gave the bride away at the wedding). Eleanor Rosalynn Smith was much better known as Rosalynn Carter, wife of 39th President Jimmy Carter.

10. ELIZABETH. Neither of the Elizabeths was known as Elizabeth. Elizabeth Virginia Wallace Truman was known as Bess, and Elizabeth Ann Bloomer Warren Ford was known as Betty. Both their husbands succeeded to the Presidency (Harry Truman upon Franklin Roosevelt's death, in 1945; Gerald Ford upon Richard Nixon's resignation, in 1974).

6. *The Most Popular States for First Ladies to Be Born*

1. NEW YORK. Though Virginia, which birthed eight Presidents, is number one on that list, New York's nine First Ladies exceed Virginia's six and outstrip the state's four Presidents:

Elizabeth Kortright Monroe (1768)

Hannah Hoes Van Buren (1783)

Abigail Powers Fillmore (1798)

Julia Gardiner Tyler (1820)

Frances Folsom Cleveland (1864)

(Anna) Eleanor Roosevelt Roosevelt (1884)

Nancy Davis Reagan (1921)

Barbara Pierce Bush (1925)

Jacqueline Lee Bouvier Kennedy (1929)

2 (tie). VIRGINIA. The birthplace of eight Presidents was also the birthplace of six First Ladies:

Martha Dandridge Custis Washington (1731)

Martha Wayles Skelton Jefferson (1748)

Rachel Donelson Robards Jackson (1767)

Letitia Christian Tyler (1790)

Ellen "Nell" Lewis Herndon Arthur (1837)

Edith Bolling Galt Wilson (1872)

2 (tie). OHIO. Second on the list of Presidential births (with seven in the 43-year span of 1822–65), Ohio is tied for second on the list of First Ladies born there, with six in a brief 30-year span:

Lucy Ware Webb Hayes (1831)

Lucretia "Crete" Rudolph Garfield (1832)

Caroline Lavinia Scott Harrison (1832)
Ida Saxton McKinley (1847)
Florence "Flossie" Mabel Kling DeWolfe Harding (1860)
Helen "Nellie" Herron Taft (1861)

4 (tie). MISSOURI. Missouri is the first state on this list not to appear on the top of the Presidential birth states list (only Harry Truman was born in Missouri):

Julia Boggs Dent Grant (1826)
Elizabeth "Bess" Virginia Wallace Truman (1885)
Jane Wyman, Ronald Reagan's first wife (1917)

4 (tie). ILLINOIS. The birthplace of only one President (Ronald Reagan in 1911), Illinois is the birthplace of three First Ladies:

Elizabeth Ann "Betty" Bloomer Warren Ford (1918)
Hillary Diane Rodham Clinton (1947)
Michelle LaVaughn Robinson Obama (1964)

6. Six states are tied, being the birthplaces of two First Ladies each:

MASSACHUSETTS: Abigail Smith Adams (1744) and Alice Hathaway Lee Roosevelt (1861)

NEW JERSEY: Anna Tuthill Symmes Harrison (1775) and Caroline Carmichael McIntosh Fillmore (1813)

TENNESSEE: Sarah Childress Polk (1803) and Eliza McCardle Johnson (1810)

GEORGIA: Ellen Louise Axson Wilson (1860) and Eleanor Rosalynn Smith Carter (1927)

IOWA: Lou Henry Hoover (1874) and Marie "Mamie" Geneva Doud Eisenhower (1896)

TEXAS: Claudia Alta "Lady Bird" Taylor Johnson (1912) and Laura Lane Welch Bush (1946)

6a. The First Ladies Born Outside the Original 13 Colonies

The First Ladies born outside the original 13 states include the entire Ohio, Missouri, and Illinois contingents (see above), as well as the two each from Tennessee, Iowa, and Texas (see above), and the following, who were each the only daughter of their state to be married to a President:

MARY TODD LINCOLN (Kentucky, 1818)

GRACE ANNA GOODHUE COOLIDGE (Vermont, 1879)

THELMA CATHERINE "PATRICIA" "PAT" RYAN NIXON (Nevada, 1912)

6b. The Foreign-Born First Lady

LOUISA CATHERINE JOHNSON, who married John Quincy Adams, was the only First Lady born outside the United States. She was born in London, England, to an American merchant and his English wife, on February 12, 1775. She met her future husband at the age of four in France (where her family had taken refuge during the Revolutionary War, and his father was representing American colonial interests).

7. The Most Popular States for First Ladies to Be Buried

1. VIRGINIA. The birthplace of six First Ladies is also the burial place of eight, including three who were born there (Martha Washington, Martha Jefferson, and Letitia Tyler):

Martha Wayles Skelton Jefferson (1782)
Martha Dandridge Custis Washington (1802)
Elizabeth Kortright Monroe (1830)
Letitia Christian Tyler (1842)
Dolley Payne Todd Madison (1849)
Julia Gardner Tyler (1889)
Helen "Nellie" Herron Taft (1943)
Jacqueline Lee Bouvier Kennedy Onassis (1994)
(Taft and Kennedy are buried with their husbands in Arlington National Cemetery.)

2. NEW YORK. The birth state of the greatest number of First Ladies (nine) is the burial state of seven:

Hannah Hoes Van Buren (1819)
Abigail Powers Fillmore (1853)
Ellen "Nell" Lewis Herndon Arthur (1880)
Caroline Carmichael McIntosh Fillmore (1881)
Julia Boggs Dent Grant (1902)
Edith Kermit Carow Roosevelt (1948)
Anna Eleanor Roosevelt Roosevelt (1962)

3. OHIO. Number two on the list of First Lady births with six, Ohio has the graves of five First Ladies:

Anna Tuthill Symmes Harrison (1864)

Lucy Ware Webb Hayes (1889)
Ida Saxton McKinley (1907)
Lucretia "Crete" Rudolph Garfield (1918)
Florence "Flossie" Mabel Kling DeWolfe Harding (1924)

4 (tie). MASSACHUSETTS. Birthplace of two First Ladies, Massachusetts is the final resting place of three:

Abigail Smith Adams (1818; she was born in the state)
Louisa Catherine Johnson Adams (1852; she was born in England)
Alice Hathaway Lee Roosevelt (1884; she was born in the state)

4 (tie). TENNESSEE. Birthplace of two First Ladies, Tennessee is the final resting place of three:

Rachel Donelson Robards Jackson (1828; she was born in Virginia)
Eliza McCardle Johnson (1876; she was born in the state)
Sarah Childress Polk (1891; she was born in the state)

8. *The First and Last First Ladies to Be Born in the 1700s, 1800s, and 1900s*

First to be born in the 1700s, first to be born at all, was MARTHA DANDRIDGE CUSTIS WASHINGTON (her husband, George, the first President, served 1789–97). She was born on June 2, 1731 (about eight months before her President-husband).

ABIGAIL POWERS FILLMORE (wife of Millard Fillmore, who served 1850–53) was the last First Lady to be born in the 1700s, when she was born on March 13, 1798.

The first First Lady to have been born in the 1800s was JULIA GARDINER TYLER, who was born July 23, 1820, and became First Lady when she married President John Tyler on June 26, 1844. She was born after her seven immediate successors.

The first child born in the 1800s to become First Lady was SARAH CHILDRESS POLK, Tyler's successor, who was born September 4, 1803.

The last child of the 1800s to serve as First Lady, MARIE "MAMIE" GENEVA DOUD EISENHOWER (served 1953–61), was born November 14, 1896.

The first 1900s baby to become First Lady was JACQUELINE LEE BOUVIER KENNEDY (served 1961–63), who was born July 28, 1929, although her six successors were all born before she was. THELMA CATHERINE "PATRICIA" "PAT" RYAN NIXON was the first born of the 1900s babies to be First Lady (she was born March 16, 1912).

9. The First and Last First Ladies to Die in the 1700s, 1800s, 1900s, and 2000s

MARTHA WAYLES SKELTON JEFFERSON was the only President's wife to die in the 1700s. She died on September 6, 1782, two months before her 34th birthday. Her death came more than 18 years before her husband became President in 1801 (indeed, it was more than four years before George Washington became the first President).

MARTHA DANDRIDGE CUSTIS WASHINGTON, the first First Lady, was the first to die after her husband's term of office and the first to die in the 1800s. Mrs. Washington (or Lady Washington, as she was called while her husband was President) died May 22, 1802, 11 days before her 71st birthday and two and a half years after George.

The last First Lady to die in the 1800s was CAROLINE LAVINIA SCOTT HARRISON, who died in the White House during her husband's term of office on October 25, 1892.

The first First Lady to survive into the 1900s was JULIA BOGGS DENT GRANT, who was First Lady from 1869 to 1877. She died on December 14, 1902.

The last death of a First Lady in the 1900s was on May 19, 1994, when JACQUELINE LEE BOUVIER KENNEDY ONASSIS died, more than 30 years after her husband was assassinated (she'd been First Lady from 1961 to 1963).

The last-serving First Lady to die in the 1900s was THELMA CATHERINE "PATRICIA" "PAT" RYAN NIXON, who was First Lady from 1969 to 1974 and died on June 22, 1993.

The first First Lady to die in the twenty-first century was CLAUDIA ALTA "LADY BIRD" TAYLOR JOHNSON, who was First Lady from 1963 to 1969. She died on July 11, 2007, aged 94, at which time she'd been a widow for more than 34 years. She outlived only one of her successors (Pat Nixon).

10. First Ladies Who Shared Birthdays

JUNE 2: Martha Dandridge Custis Washington (1731) and Helen "Nellie" Herron Taft (1861). They also shared a deathday (May 22).

JUNE 8: Ida Saxton McKinley (1847) and Barbara Pierce Bush (1925).

Several other pairs missed sharing a birthday by one day:

Louisa Catherine Johnson Adams (February 12, 1775) and Elizabeth "Bess" Virginia Wallace Truman (February 13, 1885).

Jane Means Appleton Pierce (March 12, 1806) and Abigail Powers Fillmore (March 13, 1798).

Jacqueline Lee Bouvier Kennedy Onassis (July 28, 1929) and Alice Hathaway Lee Roosevelt (July 29, 1861).

Abigail Smith Adams (November 11, 1744) and Letitia Christian Tyler (November 12, 1790).

11. First Ladies Who Shared Deathdays

MAY 22: Martha Dandridge Custis Washington (1802) and Helen "Nellie" Herron Taft (1943). They also shared a birthday (June 2), meaning that each died 11 days before her birthday (Washington would have been 71, Taft 82).

AUGUST 14: Sarah Childress Polk (1891) and her immediate successor in the White House, Margaret "Peggy" Mackall Smith Taylor (1852).

SEPTEMBER 10: Letitia Christian Tyler (1842) died during her husband's term of office. Jane Wyman, Ronald Reagan's first wife, divorced him 32 years before he became President and died in 2007.

Only one pair missed sharing a deathday by one day: Abigail Smith Adams (October 28, 1818) and Frances Folsom Cleveland (October 29, 1947).

There is also a trio of First Ladies who died within a day of each other: Julia Gardiner Tyler (July 10, 1889), Claudia Alta "Lady Bird" Taylor Johnson (July 11, 2007), and Dolley Payne Todd Madison (July 12, 1849).

12. The First Ladies Who Outlived the Greatest Number of Their Successors

This list obviously skews toward the younger First Ladies, and the two youngest are first and third on this list.

1 (tie). JULIA GARDINER TYLER. The second youngest First Lady ever, she was 27 days shy of her 24th birthday when she married President John Tyler on June 26, 1844 (he had been widowed in September 1842). She served less than one year as First Lady, leaving office on March 4, 1845. Her husband, 30 years her senior, lived until 1862. Julia died on July 10, 1889, having out-lived nine of her successors. They were: Margaret Taylor (First Lady from 1849 to 1850; she died August 14, 1852); Abigail Fillmore (1850–53; died March 30, 1853); Caroline Fillmore (married Millard Fillmore in 1858, after he left the Presidency; died August 11, 1881); Jane Pierce (1853–57; died December 2, 1863); Mary Lincoln (1861–65; died July 16, 1882); Eliza Johnson (1865–69; died January 15, 1876); Lucy Hayes (1877–81; died June 25, 1889); Ellen Arthur (she died January 12, 1880; her husband, Chester, was President from 1881 to 1885); and Alice Roosevelt (she died February 14, 1884; her husband, Theodore, was President from 1901 to 1909).

1 (tie). SARAH CHILDRESS POLK. Julia Tyler's immediate successor, she was 17 years older than Julia and died on August 14, 1891, a month before her 88th birthday (and 42 years after her husband, James Knox Polk, died). She was in the White House during her husband's one term, 1845–49). She outlived the same successors Julia Tyler did.

3. FRANCES FOLSOM CLEVELAND. The youngest First Lady was her husband's only wife. She married President Grover Cleveland on June 2, 1886, a year

into his first term as President and two months before her 22nd birthday. They left the White House on March 4, 1889, and returned four years later for his second four-year term, retiring again, for good, on March 4, 1897. Grover died on June 24, 1908, and Frances was the first Presidential widow to remarry. She died on October 29, 1947, aged 83 years, 100 days, and was buried with her President-husband. She outlived seven of her successors, who were: Caroline Harrison (who died in office on October 25, 1892); Ida McKinley (1897–1901; died May 26, 1907); Alice Roosevelt (she died February 14, 1884; her husband, Theodore, was President from 1901 to 1909); Helen Taft (1909–13; died May 22, 1943); Ellen Wilson (died in office on August 6, 1914); Florence Harding (1921–23; died November 21, 1924); and Lou Hoover (1929–33; died January 7, 1944).

4. MARY SCOTT LORD DIMMICK HARRISON. Benjamin Harrison's first wife, Caroline Lavinia Scott Harrison, died months before he left office, on October 25, 1892. She had been sick before her death, and Caroline's niece, Mary, acted as White House hostess during the end of Benjamin's term. After he left office, Benjamin and Mary fell in love and married on April 6, 1896. Mary was 25 years younger than her aunt and her new husband (and would be #4 on the list of youngest First Ladies if Benjamin had still been in office on their wedding day). He died on March 13, 1901; she lived until January 5, 1948. She outlived six wives of Presidents who came to the White House after Benjamin retired: the same list as those Frances Cleveland outlived, except for Mary's aunt Caroline.

5. LUCRETIA "CRETE" RUDOLPH GARFIELD. Lucretia turned 49 during her husband's six months in office. Her term as First Lady ended on September 19, 1881, when James died of the wounds he'd sustained in an assassination attempt two months earlier. Crete was a widow for more than 36 years and died on March 14, 1918, one month before her 86th birthday. She outlived five successors: Ellen Arthur (she died January 12, 1880; her husband, Chester, was James Garfield's Vice President and successor); Caroline Harrison (died in office on October 25, 1892);

Ida McKinley (1897–1901; died May 26, 1907); Alice Roosevelt (died February 14, 1884; her husband, Theodore, was President from 1901 to 1909); and Edith Wilson (died in office August 6, 1914).

Four First Ladies outlived four of their successors each: Dolley Madison (1809–17), Anna Harrison (1841), Julia Grant (1869–77), and Edith Roosevelt (1901–09).

Rosalynn Carter (1977–81) has outlived one of her successors (Ronald Reagan's first wife, Jane Wyman, who died September 10, 2007). The other surviving First Ladies are Nancy Reagan (1981–89), Barbara Bush (1989–93), Hillary Clinton (1993–2001), Laura Bush (2001–09), and Michelle Obama (2009–).

13. The First Ladies Who Were Older Than the Greatest Number of Their Predecessors

1. FLORENCE "FLOSSIE" MABEL KLING DEWOLFE HARDING. Born August 15, 1860, she was five years older than her husband and was born before five women whose President-husbands served before hers (Warren Harding was President from 1921 until his death in 1923). Those five were: Frances Cleveland (born July 21, 1864; First Lady from her marriage to Grover Cleveland on June 2, 1886, until he left office on March 4, 1889, and then again from 1893 to 1897); Alice Roosevelt (born July 29, 1861, she married Theodore Roosevelt, but died in 1884; he was President from 1901 to 1909); Edith Roosevelt (born August 6, 1861, she was Theodore Roosevelt's second wife and was First Lady from 1901 to 1909); Helen Taft (born June 2, 1861, she was First Lady from 1909 to 1913); and Florence's immediate predecessor, Edith Wilson (born October 15, 1872, she was the second wife of Woodrow Wilson, marrying him during his first term, on December 18, 1915, and left the White House with him on March 4, 1921).

2. ELLEN LOUISE AXSON WILSON. Born May 15, 1860, four women born after her married men who became President before Ellen's husband, Woodrow (1913–21). They were the same as those who were younger than Florence Harding (see above) except, of course, for Edith Wilson, who married Ellen's husband after her death in office, on August 6, 1914.

3 (tie). RACHEL DONELSON ROBARDS JACKSON. Born June 15, 1767, she died on December 22, 1828, 72 days before her husband was inaugurated. She was older than the three previous First Ladies: Dolley Madison (born May 20, 1768; she was First Lady from 1809 to 1817, although she also served as White House hostess for the widower Thomas Jefferson, from 1801 to

1809); Elizabeth Monroe (born June 30, 1768; she was First Lady from 1817 to 1825); and Louisa Adams (born February 12, 1775; she was First Lady from 1825 to 1829).

3 (tie). MARGARET "PEGGY" MACKALL SMITH TAYLOR. Born September 21, 1788, she was First Lady from March 4, 1849, until her husband, Zachary, died in office on July 9, 1850. She was older than her three predecessors: Letitia Tyler (born November 12, 1790; First Lady from William Henry Harrison's death on April 4, 1841, until her own death on September 10, 1842); Julia Tyler (born July 23, 1820; First Lady from the day she married President John Tyler on June 26, 1844, until he left office on March 4, 1845); and Sarah Polk (born September 4, 1803; she was First Lady from 1845 to 1849).

3 (tie). ELIZA MCCARDLE JOHNSON. Born October 4, 1810, she was First Lady from Abraham Lincoln's death on April 15, 1865, until her husband, Andrew, left office on March 4, 1869. She was older than three of her predecessors: Julia Tyler (born July 23, 1820; First Lady from the day she married President John Tyler on June 26, 1844, until he left office on March 4, 1845); Caroline Fillmore (born October 21, 1813; she married former President Millard Fillmore on February 10, 1858); and Mary Lincoln (born December 13, 1818; she was First Lady from 1861 until Abraham's death).

3 (tie). HELEN "NELLIE" HERRON TAFT. Born June 2, 1861, she was First Lady from 1909 to 1913. She was born before three women who married Presidents who served before her husband: Frances Cleveland (born July 21, 1864, she married President Grover Cleveland on June 2, 1886, and was First Lady until 1889, and then again from 1893 to 1897); Alice Roosevelt (born July 29, 1861; she died in 1884, but her husband, Theodore, was President from 1901 to 1909); and Edith Roosevelt (born August 6, 1861; she married Theodore Roosevelt after Alice's death).

3 (tie). JANE WYMAN. Born January 5, 1917 (though she claimed January 4, 1914), she was married to Ronald Reagan (who was President from 1981

to 1989) from 1940 to 1949. Three women born after her were First Lady before her ex-husband became President: Jacqueline Kennedy (born July 28, 1929; she was First Lady 1961–63); Betty Ford (born April 8, 1918; she was First Lady 1974–77); and Rosalynn Carter (born August 18, 1927; she was First Lady 1977–81).

14. The First Ladies with the Fewest Living Predecessors

MARTHA WASHINGTON (1789–97), the first First Lady, was the only one to have no living predecessors for the entirety of her term.

The First Ladies who had only one living predecessor:

1. ABIGAIL ADAMS (1797–1801). Her only predecessor, Martha Washington, died in May 1802, more than a year after Abigail moved out of the White House.

2. DOLLEY MADISON (1809–17). Her only living predecessor, Abigail Adams, died in October 1818, more than a year after Dolley moved out of the White House.

3. ELIZABETH MONROE (1817–25). Abigail Adams died October 28, 1818, leaving Elizabeth with only one living predecessor, Dolley Madison. Dolley outlived Elizabeth by 19 years.

15. The First Ladies with the Most Living Predecessors

1. HILLARY CLINTON (1993–2001) had eight living predecessors for 153 days. Jacqueline Kennedy, Lady Bird Johnson, Pat Nixon, Betty Ford, Rosalyn Carter, Nancy Reagan, Barbara Bush, and Ronald Reagan's first wife, Jane Wyman, were all alive when she moved into the White House. Pat Nixon died on June 22, 1993, and Jacqueline Kennedy died 11 months later.

2. ELEANOR ROOSEVELT (1933–45) had seven living predecessors for 10 years, 79 days. Frances Cleveland, Edith Roosevelt (her uncle's widow), Helen Taft, Edith Wilson, Grace Coolidge, Lou Hoover, and Benjamin Harrison's second wife, Mary, were all alive when she moved into the White House. Helen Taft died on May 22, 1943, and Lou Hoover on January 7, 1944.

3. LAURA BUSH (2001–09) had seven living predecessors for 6 years, 172 days: Lady Bird Johnson, Betty Ford, Rosalynn Carter, Nancy Reagan, Barbara Bush (her mother-in-law), Hillary Clinton, and Ronald Reagan's first wife, Jane Wyman. Lady Bird Johnson died on July 11, 2007, and Jane Wyman two months later, on September 10.

4. BARBARA BUSH (1989–93) had seven living predecessors for the entirety of her four-year term: Jacqueline Kennedy, Lady Bird Johnson, Pat Nixon, Betty Ford, Rosalynn Carter, Nancy Reagan, and Ronald Reagan's first wife, Jane Wyman.

5 (tie). CAROLINE HARRISON, GRACE COOLIDGE, LOU HOOVER, BESS TRUMAN, ROSALYNN CARTER, NANCY REAGAN, and MICHELLE OBAMA all had six living predecessors for at least part of their terms.

16. The Times There Were the Greatest Number of Living Current and Former First Ladies

From January 20 to June 22, 1993, there were eight living current and former First Ladies. During those six months, in addition to First Lady Hillary Clinton, the retired First Ladies were: Jacqueline Kennedy (1961–63), Lady Bird Johnson (1963–69), Pat Nixon (1969–74), Betty Ford (1974–77), Rosalynn Carter (1977–81), Nancy Reagan (1981–89), and Barbara Bush (1989–1993). On June 22, 1993, Pat Nixon, who had been in failing health for several years, died.

On eight different occasions, there were seven living current and former First Ladies.

The first time was from March 4 to June 25, 1889. That period started with Benjamin Harrison's inauguration, making Caroline Harrison First Lady, and ended when Lucy Hayes (who had been First Lady from 1877 to 1881) died. The other former First Ladies at that time were Julia Tyler (1844–45), Sarah Polk (1845–49), Julia Grant (1869–77), Lucretia Garfield (1881), and Frances Cleveland (1886–89).

From Franklin (and Eleanor) Roosevelt's inauguration on March 4, 1933, until Helen Taft's death on May 22, 1943, there were seven. The others at that time were Frances Cleveland (1886–89 and 1893–97), Edith Roosevelt (1901–09), Edith Wilson (1915–21), Grace Coolidge (1923–29), and Lou Hoover (1929–33).

From Jimmy (and Rosalynn) Carter's inauguration on January 20, 1977, until Mamie Eisenhower's death on November 1, 1979, there were seven.

The others at that time were Bess Truman (1945–53), Jacqueline Kennedy (1961–63), Lady Bird Johnson (1963–69), Pat Nixon (1969–74), and Betty Ford (1974–77).

There were six from Eisenhower's death until Ronald (and Nancy) Reagan's inauguration on January 20, 1981, which brought the number back up to seven. Bess Truman's death on October 18, 1982, again reduced the number to six. George H.W. Bush's inauguration on January 20, 1989, made his wife, Barbara, the seventh living First Lady.

Following Pat Nixon's death (see above), there were seven First Ladies from June 22, 1993, until May 19, 1994, which is when Jacqueline Kennedy died. George W. Bush's inauguration on January 20, 2001, made Laura Bush the seventh living First Lady. This period ended on July 11, 2007, when Lady Bird Johnson died.

Barack Obama's inauguration on January 20, 2009, made Michelle Obama the seventh living First Lady.

17. During Which Year Were the Greatest Number of First Ladies Born?

The 48 First Ladies were born during a 233-year span, from Martha Washington in 1731 to Michelle Obama in 1964. So on average, one First Lady was born every 4 years, 312 days. But in one span of 448 days (1860–61), five of them were born (an average of one every 3 months).

1861 was the year of three First Ladies. Successive Presidential wives Alice Roosevelt, Edith Roosevelt, and Helen Taft were all born that year, within 65 days of each other. First born was Helen Herron Taft (who was First Lady from 1909 to 1913) on June 2. Theodore Roosevelt's first wife, Alice Hathaway Lee Roosevelt, was then born on July 29 (she died in 1880), and a week later, on August 6, came Theodore Roosevelt's second wife, Edith Kermit Carow Roosevelt (who was First Lady from 1901 to 1909).

Five other years saw the births of two First Ladies each:

In 1768, Dolley Payne Todd Madison was born on May 20 (she was First Lady from 1809 to 1817), and her successor, Elizabeth Kortright Monroe was born on June 30.

In 1775, Louisa Catherine Johnson Adams was born on February 12 in London, England (1825–29), and Anna Tuthill Symmes Harrison was born on July 25 (she was First Lady for a month in 1841).

In 1832, Lucretia Rudolph Garfield was born on April 19 (she was First Lady for six months in 1881), and Caroline Lavinia Scott Harrison was born on October 1 (she died in office in 1892).

In 1860, Ellen Louise Axson Wilson was born on May 15 (she died during her husband's first term of office, in 1914), and Florence Mabel Kling DeWolfe Harding was born on August 15 (she was First Lady from 1921 until her husband's death in 1923).

In 1912, Thelma Catherine "Pat" Ryan Nixon (1969–74) was born on March 16, and her predecessor, Claudia Alta "Lady Bird" Taylor Johnson (1963–69), was born on December 22.

18. During Which Year Did the Greatest Number of First Ladies Die?

Four separate years saw the deaths of two First Ladies each:

In 1852, Louisa Catherine Johnson Adams (1825–29) died on May 15, and Margaret "Peggy" Mackall Smith Taylor (1849–50) died on August 14.

In 1889, Lucy Ware Webb Hayes (1877–81) died on June 25, and Julia Gardiner Tyler (1844–45) died 15 days later, on July 10.

In 1948, Mary Scott Lord Dimmick Harrison (who married Benjamin Harrison in 1896, after he retired from the Presidency) died on January 5, and Edith Kermit Carow Roosevelt (1901–09) died on September 30.

In 2007, Claudia Alta "Lady Bird" Taylor Johnson (1963–69) died on July 11, and Jane Wyman (who was married to Ronald Reagan from 1940 to 1949) died on September 10.

19. During Which President's Term of Office Were the Greatest Number of First Ladies Born?

Nine First Ladies were born before George Washington was inaugurated as the first President: Martha Washington, Abigail Adams, Martha Jefferson, Dolley Madison, Elizabeth Monroe, Louisa Adams, Rachel Jackson, Hannah Van Buren, and Anna Harrison. After George Washington took office, the term that saw the greatest number of First Ladies born is surprisingly not Franklin Roosevelt's term of office, which was the longest.

1. ABRAHAM LINCOLN (1861–65). During Lincoln's four years and one month, four future First Ladies were born: Helen Taft (1909–13), born June 2, 1861; Alice Roosevelt (Theodore Roosevelt's first wife, who died long before he became President), born July 29, 1861; Edith Roosevelt (1901–09), born August 6, 1861; and Frances Cleveland (1886–89, 1893–97), born July 21, 1864.

2 (tie). ANDREW JACKSON (1829–37). Jackson's eight-year term of office saw the birth of three future First Ladies: Lucy Hayes (1877–81) was born August 28, 1831; Lucretia Garfield (1881) was born April 19, 1832; and Caroline Harrison (1889–92) was born October 1, 1832.

2 (tie). JAMES BUCHANAN (1857–61). Buchanan's four-year term of office saw the birth of three future Presidential wives: Mary Harrison (married Benjamin Harrison three years after he left office), born April 30, 1858; Ellen Wilson (1913–14), born May 15, 1860; and Florence Harding (1921–23), born August 15, 1860.

Nine Presidencies saw the births of two future First Ladies each: George Washington (Margaret Taylor and Letitia Tyler); Thomas Jefferson (Sarah Polk and Jane Pierce); James Madison (Eliza Johnson and Caroline Fillmore); James Monroe (Mary Lincoln and Julia Tyler); Ulysses Grant (Edith Wilson and Lou Hoover); William Taft (Pat Nixon and Lady Bird Johnson); Woodrow Wilson (Jane Wyman Reagan and Betty Ford); Calvin Coolidge (Barbara Bush and Rosalynn Carter); and Harry Truman (Laura Bush and Hillary Clinton). In addition, two future First Ladies were born while Grover Cleveland was President: Bess Truman during his first term (1885–89) and Mamie Eisenhower during his second (1893–97).

20. During Which President's Term of Office Did the Greatest Number of First Ladies Die?

1. BENJAMIN HARRISON (1889–93). During Harrison's one four-year term, four First Ladies died: Lucy Ware Webb Hayes (1877–81) died June 25, 1889; Julia Gardiner Tyler (1844–45) died July 10, 1889; Sarah Childress Polk (1845–49) died August 14, 1891; and Harrison's own wife, Caroline Lavinia Scott Harrison, died October 25, 1892, days before Harrison lost his bid for reelection.

2. HARRY TRUMAN (1945–53). During Truman's almost eight years in the Presidency, three former First Ladies died: Frances Folsom Cleveland (1886–89 and 1893–97) died October 29, 1947; Mary Scott Lord Dimmick Harrison (who married Benjamin Harrison in 1896, after he left the Presidency) died January 5, 1948; and Edith Kermit Carow Roosevelt (1901–09) died September 30, 1948.

Ten Presidencies saw the deaths of two First Ladies each: James Monroe (Abigail Adams and Hannah Van Buren); Millard Fillmore (Louisa Adams and Margaret Taylor); Abraham Lincoln (Jane Pierce and Anna Harrison); Chester Arthur (Mary Lincoln and Alice Roosevelt); Theodore Roosevelt (Julia Grant and Ida McKinley); Woodrow Wilson (his first wife, Ellen Wilson, and Lucretia Garfield); Franklin Roosevelt (Helen Taft and Lou Hoover); John Kennedy (Edith Wilson and Eleanor Roosevelt); Bill Clinton (Pat Nixon and Jacqueline Kennedy); and George W. Bush (Lady Bird Johnson and Jane Wyman Reagan).

21. The Longest Periods of Time during Which No First Ladies Died

1. September 6, 1782, to May 22, 1802; 19 years, 258 days. The time between the first death of a President's wife (Martha Jefferson, who died more than 18 years before her husband, Thomas, became President) and the death of the first President's wife (Martha Washington, who died two and a half years after her husband George).

2. November 21, 1924, to May 22, 1943; 18 years, 182 days. The time between the deaths of Florence Harding (who was First Lady from 1921 until her husband's death in 1923) and Helen Taft (who was First Lady from 1909 to 1913 and the wife of the Chief Justice of the United States from 1921 to 1930).

3. November 7, 1962, to November 1, 1979; 16 years, 359 days. The time between the deaths of Eleanor Roosevelt (who was First Lady for the longest period of time, 1933 to 1945) and Mamie Eisenhower (who was First Lady from 1953 to 1961).

4. May 22, 1802, to October 28, 1818; 16 years, 159 days. The time between the deaths of the first two First Ladies, Martha Washington and Abigail Adams.

5. May 19, 1994, to July 11, 2007; 13 years, 53 days. The time between the deaths of Jacqueline Kennedy (who was First Lady from 1961 to 1963) and her immediate successor, Lady Bird Johnson (who was First Lady from 1963 to 1969). Kennedy remarried after her husband John's assassination; her second husband, Aristotle Onassis, also predeceased her. Johnson was a widow for more than 34 years.

THE FIRST LADIES: ON THE JOB

22. First (and Second) Ladies Who Were College Graduates

Thirteen of the women who married Presidents were college graduates.

1. LUCY WARE WEBB HAYES (1831–89) was the first First Lady to graduate from college. She graduated from Wesleyan Women's College in Ohio in 1850 and was First Lady from 1877 to 1881.

2. FRANCES FOLSOM CLEVELAND (1864–1947). Her father and Grover Cleveland were law partners, but when Oscar Folsom died, Cleveland took responsibility for Frances and her mother. His guardianship turned into a more personal relationship while she was a student at Wells College. She graduated in 1885 and the next year married President Cleveland to become the youngest First Lady ever, from 1886 to 1889, and again from 1893 to 1897.

3. CAROLINE LAVINIA SCOTT HARRISON (1832–92) graduated from Oxford Female Institute, a school her father founded, in Ohio, and was First Lady from 1889 to 1892.

4. HELEN "NELLIE" HERRON TAFT (1861–1943) was a graduate of the Cincinnati College of Music and then a music teacher before marrying William Howard Taft. She was First Lady from 1909 to 1913.

5. GRACE ANNA GOODHUE COOLIDGE (1879–1957) graduated from the University of Vermont in 1902 and was a lip-reading teacher at the Clarke Institute for the Deaf in Massachusetts when she married Calvin Coolidge in 1905. She was First Lady from 1923 to 1929.

6. LOU HENRY HOOVER (1874–1944) met Herbert Hoover at Stanford University, when she was a freshman and he a senior (they were both geology majors). They decided to hold off their marriage until she graduated, which she did in 1898. They married in January 1899, and she was First Lady from 1929 to 1933.

7. JACQUELINE LEE BOUVIER KENNEDY ONASSIS (1929–94) was a graduate of George Washington University in Washington, DC (1951), after attending Vassar College and the Sorbonne. She was a photographer when she met and married John Kennedy. She was First Lady from 1961 to 1963.

8. CLAUDIA ALTA "LADY BIRD" TAYLOR JOHNSON (1912–2007) graduated from St. Mary's Episcopal College for Women (in Texas) in 1930 and then decided to attend the University of Texas. From the latter school she received two BAs, in 1933 and 1934, with high honors. She married Lyndon Johnson at the end of 1934 and was First Lady from 1963 to 1969.

9. THELMA CATHERINE "PAT" RYAN NIXON (1912–93) graduated with a BS in merchandising from the University of Southern California in 1937. She also received a high-school teaching certificate, which the school considered the equivalent to a Master's degree. She was teaching at Whittier (California) High School when she met Richard Nixon and then married him in 1940. She was First Lady from 1969 to 1974.

10. NANCY DAVIS REAGAN (born Anne Francis Robbins in 1921) graduated from Smith College in Massachusetts in 1943, with a degree in drama. In 1946, she appeared on stage on Broadway and, in 1949, signed a film contract with MGM. That same year, she met Ronald Reagan, whom she married in 1952. She was First Lady from 1981 to 1989.

11. HILLARY DIANNE RODHAM CLINTON (1947–) received her BA from Wellesley College in 1969, where her classmates chose her as the commencement speaker. She met Bill Clinton at Yale Law School, where she earned a JD in 1973. She married Clinton in 1975 and was First Lady from 1993 to 2001. In 2000, she became the first First Lady to be elected to office in her own right, when she was elected to the Senate, representing New York. She was reelected in 2006, and in 2009, she became the first First Lady to serve in the Cabinet, when Barack Obama appointed her the 67th Secretary of State.

12. LAURA LANE WELCH BUSH (1946–) received a BS from Southern Methodist University (Texas) in 1968 and was a teacher. She then earned an MS in Library Science from the University of Texas at Austin in 1973. She met and married George W. Bush in 1977, had twin daughters in 1981, and was First Lady from 2001 to 2009.

13. MICHELLE LAVAUGHN ROBINSON OBAMA (1964–) received a BA from Princeton University in 1985 and a JD from Harvard Law School in 1988. She met Barack Obama when they worked for the same law firm in Chicago and married him in 1992. She became First Lady in 2009.

Though fewer in number, the college-graduate wives of the Vice Presidents also have some impressive degrees:

1. GRACE COOLIDGE (see above).

2. MURIEL FAY BUCK HUMPHREY BROWN (1912–98) was a graduate of Huron College. She married Hubert Humphrey in 1936 and was Second Lady

from 1965 to 1969. After leaving the Vice Presidency, Humphrey was again elected to the Senate from Minnesota (he had been a Senator before becoming Vice President). When he died in January 1978, Muriel was appointed to his Senate seat, becoming the first wife of a Vice President to hold public office. She was a Senator from January 25 to November 7, 1978, but chose not to run for a term of her own. In 1979, she married Max Brown.

3. PAT NIXON (see above).

4. LADY BIRD JOHNSON (see above).

5. JOAN ADAMS MONDALE (1930–) received her BA from Macalester College. She married Walter Mondale in 1955 and was Second Lady from 1977 to 1981.

6. MARILYN TUCKER QUAYLE (1949–) received her BS from Purdue University and her JD from the Indiana University School of Law in Indianapolis. In 1972, she married Dan Quayle, and the husband-and-wife team opened their own law practice. They dissolved it when he was elected to the Senate. When he became Vice President in 1989, she was offered the appointment to his now-vacant Senate seat, but declined, citing potential conflicts of interest.

7. MARY ELIZABETH "TIPPER" AITCHESON GORE (1948–) received her BA from Boston University in 1970 (the same year she married Al Gore) and her MA from George Peabody College in 1975. She famously testified before Congress over explicit lyrics in recorded music while her husband was a Senator representing Tennessee. She was Second Lady from 1993 to 2001.

8. LYNNE ANN VINCENT CHENEY (1941–) received her BA from Colorado College, her MA from the University of Colorado at Boulder, and her PhD from the University of Wisconsin at Madison. She married Dick Cheney in 1964 and was a professional author before (and after) her husband was elected Vice President. She was the Second Lady from 2001 to 2009.

9. JILL TRACY JACOBS BIDEN (1951–) received her BA from the University of Delaware in 1975. She was a teacher when she married Senator Joe Biden in 1977. Later, she continued her education and earned an MEd from West Chester University in 1981, an MA from Villanova University in 1987, and at the age of 56, an EdD from the University of Delaware in 2007. Her husband was elected Vice President in 2008.

23. The Only First Lady to Hold Elective Office in Her Own Right

Many First Ladies are almost partners with their President-husbands, acting as sounding boards, unofficial ambassadors, or whatever is needed. Eleanor Roosevelt represented her husband, Franklin, acting as his eyes and ears on the ground throughout the country, since his mobility was limited. After his death, Harry Truman appointed her US Delegate to the United Nations, giving her an official government position in her own name. And it's generally assumed that for six months after Woodrow Wilson's 1919 stroke, Edith Wilson was acting President.

But only one First Lady has been elected to public office: Hillary Clinton. Bill Clinton and Hillary Rodham met while they were both students at Yale Law School. She moved to Arkansas to be with him. While he was Governor of Arkansas, she headed the state's education standards committee (while also working as a litigator for a private law firm).

Early in the Presidential campaign of 1992, Bill and Hillary Clinton presented themselves to the electorate as a kind of co-Presidency, offering "two for the price of one," but the public never warmed to that proposal, and it was dropped. She did, however, play a major role in her husband's administration: taking part in the selection of Cabinet members, heading the Task Force on National Health Care Reform early in his administration, and occupying an office in the West Wing.

Late in his second term, it became clear that she wanted something more than to be the former First Lady. When New York Senator Daniel Patrick Moynihan announced his retirement, the Clintons bought a house in New York state. With the backing of the Democratic Party, and Moynihan's enthusiastic support, Hillary Clinton easily won the election in her newly adopted state over the largely unknown county executive Rick Lazio. She was sworn in on January 3, 2001, the first First Lady to be elected to office on her own. For 17 days, she was both the junior Senator from New York and the First Lady of the United States.

In 2006, she was easily reelected, and in 2008, she sought the Democratic nomination for President. In a long, hard-fought, and ultimately very close race, she came in second to Senator Barack Obama of Illinois (who had won his first term in the Senate in 2004). After Obama won the election, he appointed Hillary Clinton Secretary of State, making her the first First Lady to be in the official line of succession to the Presidency (behind the Vice President, Speaker of the House, and President *pro tempore* of the Senate).

Six Presidents had previously served as Secretary of State—Thomas Jefferson, James Madison, James Monroe, John Quincy Adams, Martin Van Buren, and James Buchanan—two others had served in the Cabinet (William Howard Taft was Secretary of War, and Herbert Hoover was Secretary of Commerce). Several Vice Presidents served in the Senate after their terms as Vice President, but only two moved into the Cabinet (John C. Calhoun, who was later Secretary of State, and Henry A. Wallace, who was Secretary of Agriculture, Vice President, and then Secretary of Commerce). Andrew Johnson served briefly in the Senate after his Presidency. Hillary Clinton, however, is the first person to have lived in the White House and then become Secretary of State.

She served Barack Obama's first term as Secretary of State and then resigned from the position for his second term. In early 2015 she officially announced her candidacy for the Presidency once again and at the end of the year, was the prohibitive front-runner for the Democratic nomination.

24. The Five Oldest First Ladies

Based on the First Ladies' ages when their husbands took office, the list runs as follows:

1. ANNA HARRISON was 65 years, 222 days old when her husband, William Henry Harrison, took office on March 4, 1841. The weather was bad (which lead to his illness and sudden death), and Mrs. Harrison planned to join her husband in Washington later in the spring. His death one month later meant she never had the chance to live in the White House as First Lady. To best her record, the Presidential spouse who moves into the White House following the election of 2016 will have to have been born prior to June 12, 1951.

2. BARBARA BUSH was 63 years, 226 days old when her husband, George H.W. Bush, became President on January 20, 1989. She had lived at the Naval Observatory as the wife of the Vice President for eight years prior to moving to the White House. She is also the first former First Lady to live long enough to see her son become President.

3. FLORENCE HARDING was 60 years, 201 days old when Warren G. Harding became President on March 4, 1921.

4. MARGARET "PEGGY" TAYLOR was 60 years, 166 days old when Zachary Taylor took the oath of office on March 4, 1849.

5. ELIZABETH "BESS" TRUMAN was 60 years, 58 days old when Franklin Roosevelt died and her husband, Vice President Harry Truman, became President on April 12, 1945. To knock her off the list, the person whose spouse wins the election of 2016 will have to have been born before November 23, 1956.

However, if we consider the age at the time the President left office, Bess Truman moves into first place (she was 67 years, 341 days old when Harry retired, because by far, her husband served the longest term of all those on the list). Barbara Bush maintains second place at 67 years, 226 days. Nancy Reagan would move into third place at 67 years, 198 days, because her husband, Ronald Reagan, served a full eight years as President. Martha Washington, the first First Lady, was 65 years, 256 days old when George Washington proved that a national leader could retire, on March 4, 1797. And Anna Harrison drops to fifth place, aged 65 years, 253 days when William Henry Harrison died a month after taking office.

25. The Five Youngest First Ladies

While the Constitution requires that the President be at least 35 years old, there are no qualifications for a President's spouse to be First Lady.

1 (and 3). FRANCES CLEVELAND was 21 years, 316 days old when she married bachelor President Grover Cleveland on June 2, 1886, in the White House, becoming the youngest First Lady ever. After he lost the election of 1888 to Benjamin Harrison, the Clevelands left the White House. Following Cleveland's comeback victory over Harrison in 1892, Frances Cleveland became the third-youngest woman to become First Lady when they moved back into the White House on March 4, 1893 (she was 28 years, 226 days old).

2. JULIA TYLER was 24 years, 337 days old when she married widowed President John Tyler on June 26, 1844, becoming the youngest First Lady at that time.

4 (or 3, if we discount Frances Cleveland's second term). JACQUELINE KENNEDY was the youngest woman to have been married to her President-husband before he became President. She was 31 years, 176 days old when John Kennedy took office on January 20, 1961.

5 (or 4). EDITH ROOSEVELT was 40 years, 39 days old when her husband succeeded to the Presidency upon William McKinley's assassination. Theodore Roosevelt became the youngest President ever on September 14, 1901.

6 (or 5). DOLLEY MADISON was 40 years, 297 days old when James Madison became President on March 4, 1809, but she had served as White House hostess for his predecessor, Thomas Jefferson (who was a widower), while James was Secretary of State. In order to knock her off this list, the First Lady who moves into the White House following the election of 2016 will have to have been born after March 29, 1976.

26. The First Ladies Who Were the Greatest Number of Years Older Than Their Predecessors

1. CAROLINE HARRISON was 31 years, 293 days older than Frances Cleveland. Harrison was born October 1, 1832, and was First Lady from 1889 to 1892 (she died in office). Cleveland was born July 21, 1864, and was First Lady from 1886 to 1889 (and again from 1893 to 1897).

2. IDA MCKINLEY was 17 years, 43 days older than Frances Cleveland. McKinley was born June 8, 1847, and was First Lady from 1897 to 1901. Cleveland was born July 21, 1864, and was First Lady from 1893 to 1897 (she had previously been First Lady from 1886 to 1889).

3. SARAH POLK was 16 years, 322 days older than Julia Tyler. Polk was born September 4, 1803, and was First Lady from 1845 to 1849. Tyler was born July 23, 1820, and was First Lady from 1844 to 1845.

4. LADY BIRD JOHNSON was 16 years, 218 days older than Jacqueline Kennedy. Johnson was born December 22, 1912, and was First Lady from 1963 to 1969. Kennedy was born July 28, 1929, and was First Lady from 1961 to 1963.

5. MARGARET TAYLOR was 14 years, 348 days older than Sarah Polk. Taylor was born September 21, 1788, and was First Lady from 1849 to 1850. Polk was born September 4, 1803, and was First Lady from 1845 to 1849.

27. The First Ladies Who Were the Greatest Number of Years Younger Than Their Predecessors

This list runs to more than five, because some of the people on it were not married to their President-husbands when they were in office. On the roster of Presidential spouses, the top five are numbers 1, 3, 4, 5, and 6, but on the roster of First Ladies, we would count numbers 1, 2, 3, 6, and 8.

1. JACQUELINE KENNEDY was 32 years, 256 days younger than Mamie Eisenhower. Kennedy was born July 28, 1929, and was First Lady from 1961 until her husband's death in office in 1963. Eisenhower was born November 14, 1896, and was First Lady from 1953 to 1961.

2. FRANCES CLEVELAND was 31 years, 293 days younger than Caroline Harrison. Cleveland was born July 21, 1864, and was First Lady from 1893 to 1897 (after previously having been First Lady from 1886 to 1889). Harrison was born October 1, 1832, and was First Lady from 1889 to 1892 (she died in office). Five years after Caroline Harrison died, her husband remarried, so there is another Presidential spouse in between Caroline and Frances, but at the time, Frances was Caroline's successor.

3. JULIA TYLER was 29 years, 253 days younger than Letitia Tyler. Julia was born July 23, 1820, and married the widowed President John Tyler on June 26, 1844, to become First Lady (they left office in 1845). Letitia, Tyler's first wife, was born November 12, 1790, and was First Lady from 1841 until her death on September 10, 1842.

4. FRANCES CLEVELAND was 26 years, 325 days younger than Ellen Arthur. Cleveland was born July 21, 1864, and was First Lady from June 2, 1886

(when she married President Grover Cleveland), until 1889. Arthur was born August 30, 1837, but died in 1880, a year and a half before her husband, Chester Arthur, became President (he served 1881–85).

5. MARY HARRISON was 25 years, 211 days younger than her aunt, Caroline Harrison. Mary was born April 30, 1858, and married retired President Benjamin Harrison in 1896. Caroline was born October 1, 1832, and was First Lady from 1889 until her death in late 1892, at the end of her husband President Benjamin Harrison's term.

6. HILLARY CLINTON is 22 years, 140 days younger than Barbara Bush. Clinton was born October 26, 1947, and was First Lady from 1993 to 2001. Bush was born June 8, 1925, and was First Lady from 1989 to 1993.

7. DOLLEY MADISON was 19 years, 202 days younger than Martha Jefferson. Madison was born May 20, 1768, and was First Lady from 1809 to 1817 (she had also helped President Thomas Jefferson with White House hostessing duties from 1801 to 1809). Jefferson was born October 30, 1748, and died in 1782. Her husband, President Thomas Jefferson, was in office from 1801 to 1809.

8. GRACE COOLIDGE was 18 years, 141 days younger than Florence Harding. Coolidge was born January 3, 1879, and was First Lady from 1923 to 1929. Harding was born August 15, 1860, and was First Lady from 1921 until her husband's death in office in 1923.

28. The First Ladies Who Served the Longest Terms

Twelve of the Presidents have served eight years (or more) as President, but only six Vice Presidents have served two complete terms. First Ladies, interestingly, don't exactly line up with the Presidents. To wit, eight have served eight years as First Lady: Dolley Madison (1809–17); Elizabeth Monroe (1817–25); Julia Grant (1869–77); Eleanor Roosevelt (1933–45—she was the longest-serving First Lady, as her husband was the longest-serving President); Mamie Eisenhower (1953–61); Nancy Reagan (1981–89); Hillary Clinton (1993–2001); and Laura Bush (2001–09).

Martha Washington was the first President's wife, but he took office on April 30, 1789, cutting his first term short by nearly two months. She was First Lady until March 4, 1797.

Two-term Presidents Thomas Jefferson and Andrew Jackson were widowers during their Administrations. Grover Cleveland, whose terms were non-consecutive, married Frances during his first term. Woodrow Wilson's first wife died during his first term, and he remarried while in office.

29. The First Ladies
Who Served the Shortest Terms

Looking at the Presidents' records, the first two on this list are obvious. But the First Ladies' tenures are dependent not only on their President-husbands, but also on themselves.

1. ANNA HARRISON. She was the oldest First Lady, and her husband was the oldest President elected to that point. He was also the first to die in office. He (and she) had a 31-day term, from March 4 to April 4, 1841. The weather that March was bad, and Anna told William she'd join him in Washington later in the Spring. She never did. She is the only First Lady to never make it to the national capital during her husband's term.

2. LUCRETIA GARFIELD. Her husband, James, was the second President to be assassinated. Unlike the first (Abraham Lincoln), he did not die quickly, but lingered for more than two months after being shot on July 2, 1881 (he was waiting at the train station to visit Lucretia, who was herself ill and resting in New Jersey). He finally succumbed on September 19, 1881. Their terms of office were 199 days.

3. JULIA TYLER. The first First Lady on this list for happier reasons, she was a month shy of her 24th birthday when she married President John Tyler on June 26, 1844. He had been widowed 21 months earlier. Julia and John were together through the end of his Presidency, which meant her First Lady-ship lasted 251 days. After they retired to his home in Virginia, they had seven children. He died in 1862, and she in 1889.

4. MARGARET TAYLOR. Her husband, Zachary, was the second President to die in office. While William Harrison died due to the cold he caught

in cold weather, Zachary Taylor died of a bout of gastroenteritis brought on by very hot weather, at Independence Day celebrations. He died on July 9, 1850, after the Taylors had lived in the White House for one year, 127 days.

5. ELLEN WILSON. The first on the list to predecease her husband, Ellen is the last First Lady to die in office. After marrying off two of her daughters in White House weddings, she succumbed to Bright's disease at the age of 54, on August 6, 1914. She was First Lady for one year, 155 days.

6. LETITIA TYLER. She just misses the top five. Letitia was the first First Lady to die in office. Her husband, John, was the first Vice President to succeed to the Presidency, when William Harrison died on April 4, 1841. Letitia had a paralytic stroke a few years earlier and was an invalid during her husband's Administration. She suffered a second stroke and died on September 10, 1842. She'd been First Lady for one year, 159 days.

30. Official White House Hostesses

Today, the First Lady also serves as the official White House hostess, organizing ceremonies and functions, such as state dinners (or, today, overseeing the efforts of the staff doing so), and that's the way it's been for most of the country's history. There were times, however, when the serving President was without a spouse (in most cases, their wives died while they were in office or before they took office, though James Buchanan was a lifelong bachelor, and Grover Cleveland first married during his first term). In other cases, the President's spouse was unable or unwilling to take on those hostessing duties, and others served in her stead. Presidential daughters, sisters, and other relatives have served as White House hostess:

Name	Birth Date	Tenure	Relation to President	Death Date
Martha Jefferson Randolph	September 27, 1772	March 4, 1801–March 4, 1809	Thomas Jefferson's daughter	October 10, 1836
Emily Donelson	June 1, 1807	March 4, 1829–December 19, 1836	Andrew Jackson's niece	December 19, 1836
Sarah Jackson	July 16, 1803	November 26, 1834–March 4, 1837	Andrew Jackson's daughter-in-law	August 23, 1887
Angelica Van Buren	February 13, 1818	January 1, 1839–March 4, 1841	Martin Van Buren's daughter-in-law	December 29, 1877
Jane Irwin Harrison	July 23, 1804	March 4–April 4, 1841	William Henry Harrison's daughter-in-law	May 11, 1846
Priscilla Tyler	June 14, 1816	September 10, 1842–June 26, 1844	John Tyler's daughter-in-law	December 29, 1889
Harriet Lane	May 9, 1830	March 4, 1857–March 4, 1861	James Buchanan's niece	July 3, 1903
Mary Arthur McElroy	July 5, 1841	September 19, 1881–March 4, 1885	Chester Arthur's sister	January 8, 1917

Name	Birth Date	Tenure	Relation to President	Death Date
Rose Cleveland	June 13, 1846	March 4, 1885– June 2, 1886	Grover Cleveland's sister	November 22, 1918
Mary Harrison McKee	April 3, 1858	October 25, 1892– March 4, 1893	Benjamin Harrison's daughter	October 28, 1930
Margaret Woodrow Wilson	April 16, 1886	August 6, 1914– December 18, 1915	Woodrow Wilson's daughter	February 12, 1944

MARTHA WASHINGTON "PATSY" JEFFERSON RANDOLPH (September 27, 1772–October 10, 1836) was the older of Thomas Jefferson's two daughters to survive to adulthood. Born at Monticello, she was often her father's companion after her mother's death, including living in France while he was US Minister. After returning to the United States, she married Thomas Mann Randolph, Jr., in 1790. He served in the House of Representatives (1803–07) and as Governor of Virginia (1819–22). They had 12 children together. Martha educated her children at home and was engrossed with caring for her large family, so she was unable to spend all her time at the White House when her father was President (though in those days, the President only spent perhaps half the year in the capital). She visited with her husband and children in 1802, with her sister Mary in 1803, and during the winter of 1805/1806.

When she was not available, Dolley Madison (the wife of James Madison, who was at the time Secretary of State) filled in as White House hostess.

After Thomas Jefferson's retirement, and Martha's separation from her husband, she devoted much of her life to his declining years. Jefferson describes her as the "cherished companion of his youth and the nurse of his old age."

Her children included:

- Thomas Jefferson Randolph (1792–1875), who served in the Virginia House of Delegates, was rector of the University of Virginia, and was a colonel in the Confederate Army during the Civil War.

- Meriwether Lewis Randolph (1810–37), whose widow, Elizabeth Martin, remarried Andrew Jackson Donelson, a nephew of President Andrew Jackson.
- George Wythe Randolph (1818–67), who was the third Secretary of War of the Confederate States of America (March–November 1862).

EMILY DONELSON (June 1, 1807–December 19, 1836) was born on her father's farm in Donelson, Tennessee. Her father, John Donelson, was the brother of Rachel Donelson Jackson, the wife of future President Andrew Jackson. In 1824, Emily married A.J. Donelson, who was her first cousin and a ward of Andrew and Rachel Jackson.

After the election of 1828, before Rachel Jackson's death, the Jacksons had apparently planned to have Emily accompany them to Washington to assist in the duties of White House hostess (they had operated under a similar arrangement at The Hermitage, their plantation in Tennessee). Rachel Jackson's death changed the plans, and the President-elect asked Emily to take over all the responsibilities of the White House hostess, which she did with the aid of her niece, Mary Ann Eastin.

She arrived in Washington at the age of 21, and her husband, A.J. Donelson, served as President Jackson's private secretary.

The Petticoat Affair, a society scandal involving Secretary of War John Henry Eaton and his new wife, Peggy, divided Washington society. Emily was on the side of shunning the Eatons, but the President—perhaps remembering the difficulties that surrounded his own wife's past—favored ignoring the scandal and welcoming the Eatons. The rift between Andrew and Emily grew, and came to a head in the summer of 1830, during a visit home. Emily refused to stay at Jackson's Hermitage, and when he returned to the capital later that year, A.J. accompanied him, but Emily did not. She was estranged from the President for more than a year, though they eventually reconciled. She died of tuberculosis in 1836.

SARAH YORKE JACKSON (July 16, 1803–August 23, 1887) was born in Philadelphia to a wealthy family. Her father died in 1815, and her mother in 1820. She and her two sisters were then raised by their aunts.

Sarah married Andrew Jackson, Jr., the adopted son of the President, in Philadelphia on November 24, 1831. After an extended honeymoon at the White House, they returned to The Hermitage, which they managed until a fire destroyed much of the main house in 1834. They and their two young children then moved into the White House, arriving on November 26, 1834. (They went on to have five children, though only three lived to adulthood.)

Sarah immediately took on the role of co-hostess of the White House, but Jackson referred to her as the "mistress of the Hermitage" rather than White House hostess, apparently to avoid causing any friction between Sarah and Emily. Sarah took over all the duties as White House hostess after Emily's death. She remained with the President until the end of his term, other than trips home to oversee the reconstruction. She lived at the plantation with her husband and father-in-law until his death in 1845. Shortly before the Civil War, they moved to Mississippi.

SARAH ANGELICA SINGLETON VAN BUREN (February 13, 1818–December 29, 1877) was born in Wedgefield, South Carolina, a cousin of Dolley Madison. Known as Angelica, she married Abraham Van Buren (the eldest son of the President, who was 11 years her senior) on November 27, 1838. On New Year's Day, 1839, she assumed the duties of hostess at the White House. In the spring of that year, Angelica and Abraham took an extended trip through Europe. When they returned that autumn, she resumed her duties at the White House for the rest of her father-in-law's Presidency.

After Martin Van Buren's defeat in 1840, Angelica and Abraham lived at the Van Buren home of Lindenwald, in Kinderhook, New York, wintering at her family home in South Carolina. From 1848 until her death, she lived in New York City.

JANE IRWIN HARRISON (July 23, 1804–May 11, 1846) was born in Pennsylvania. She married William Henry Harrison's fourth son, William Henry Harrison, Jr., and had three children with him. He died in 1838. In 1840, her father-in-law was elected President. In early 1841, First Lady Anna Harrison decided to stay home in Ohio until the weather improved later in the Spring. Instead, Jane traveled with the new President to serve as his hostess, assisted by her 73-year-old aunt, Jane Irwin Findlay.

Jane Irwin Harrison's sister, Elizabeth Ramsey Irwin (1810–50), married John Scott Harrison (William Henry Harrison, Jr.'s next younger brother) in 1831 and was the mother of President Benjamin Harrison.

ELIZABETH PRISCILLA COOPER TYLER (June 14, 1816–December 29, 1889) was born in New York City. Known as Priscilla, she was the daughter of actor Thomas Apthorpe Cooper and began her own acting career at the age of 17. The Cooper family was very successful, but their fortunes reversed during the Panic of 1837.

While playing Desdemona in a production of *Othello* in Richmond, Virginia, she met John Tyler's eldest son, Robert. They married in September 1839 and then moved to Virginia to live with Robert's family.

In 1839, Tyler's wife, Letitia, suffered a paralytic stroke that left her an invalid. After Tyler's succession to the Presidency, Letitia remained in the upstairs living quarters of the White House; she came downstairs to the public level only once, to attend the wedding of her daughter, Elizabeth (1823–50), in January 1842. Letitia died on September 10, 1842.

Due to Letitia's illness, Priscilla assisted the President as White House hostess, and in June 1843, Priscilla became the first woman acting as First Lady to travel with the President as an official member of the Presidential party, when they traveled to Boston for the dedication of the Bunker Hill Monument.

On June 26, 1844, John Tyler became the first President to marry while in office, and his new bride, Julia Gardiner Tyler, became First Lady and replaced Priscilla as White House hostess. Priscilla and Robert Tyler moved to Philadelphia, where they lived until the Civil War broke out. They lived in Virginia during the war, where Robert served as register of the Treasury of the Confederacy. After the war, they settled in Montgomery, Alabama, and Robert regained his fortunes as a lawyer, editor of the *Montgomery Advertiser*, and leader of the state Democratic Party. After his death in 1877, Priscilla remained in Montgomery until her death.

HARRIET REBECCA LANE (later Johnston) (May 9, 1830–July 3, 1903) was the youngest child of Elliott Tole Lane, a merchant, and Jane Ann Buchanan Lane. Her mother died when she was nine, and her father two years later. She asked that her favorite uncle, James Buchanan, be appointed her legal guardian.

In 1854, Harriet joined Buchanan in London, where he was US Minister to the Court of St. James. Queen Victoria gave Harriet the rank of ambassador's wife. When Buchanan was elected President, Harriet naturally joined him in the White House. She was a popular hostess and a style icon: women copied her hair and clothing styles (especially when she lowered the neckline on her inaugural gown by two inches), and a popular song ("Listen to the Mockingbird") was dedicated to her. While in the White House, she used her position to promote social causes, such as improving the living conditions of Native Americans in reservations. She also made a point of inviting artists and musicians to White House functions.

Harriet waited until she was almost 36 to marry Baltimore banker Henry Elliott Johnston. By 1884, she was a widow, and both her young sons were dead. She lived her final years in Washington and acquired a sizable art collection that she bequeathed to the Smithsonian Institution. She also endowed a home for invalid children at the Johns Hopkins Hospital in Baltimore, known as the Harriet Lane Outpatient Clinics.

The US Revenue Cutter *Harriet Lane* (in service 1861–81) was named for her. So too were the US Coast Guard Cutter *Harriet Lane*, WSC-141 (1926–46), and the still-active USCGC *Harriet Lane*, WMEC-903 (commissioned in 1984).

MARY ARTHUR MCELROY (July 5, 1841–January 8, 1917) was the 12-years-younger sister of President Chester Arthur. Born in Greenwich, New York, she was the last of the nine Arthur children (Chester was the fifth). In 1861, she married insurance salesman John McElroy (1833–1915). They lived in Albany and had four children.

When Chester succeeded to the Presidency in September 1881, he asked Mary to care for his young daughter, Ellen, and act as "Mistress of the White House." But because she had her own family in Albany, Mary lived in

Washington only during the busy winter social season. Although Arthur never officially granted her the protocol of a formal position, she was a popular and competent hostess. Her oldest daughter, May, and Chester's daughter, Nell, often assisted her in presiding over social functions in the White House.

ROSE ELIZABETH CLEVELAND (June 13, 1846–November 22, 1918) was the nine-years-younger sister of Grover Cleveland. Like the Arthurs before them, the President was the fifth of nine children, and his sister-hostess, the youngest.

Rose was a teacher and a scholar, and also cared for her widowed mother for many years (until her death in 1882). When Grover was elected President, Rose stood by him during his inauguration and lived in the White House for two years. As an intellectual, Rose Cleveland did not completely fit into Washington high society and was apparently more comfortable lecturing than entertaining.

When Grover married Frances Folsom on June 2, 1886, Rose left the White House and resumed her career in education. She became the principal of the Collegiate Institute of Lafayette, Indiana, a writer and lecturer, and the editor of the Chicago-based magazine *Literary Life*. She died during the 1918 flu pandemic.

Rose published a volume of lectures and essays under the title *George Eliot's Poetry, and other Studies* (1885), and a novel titled *The Long Run* (1886). She co-authored *How to Win: A Book for Girls* (1887) with suffragist Frances Elizabeth Willard and wrote the introduction for *Social Mirror: A Complete Treatise on the Laws, Rules and Usages that Govern our Most Refined Homes and Social Circles*. She also translated *The Soliloquies of St. Augustine* (1910), for which she wrote a lengthy introduction and extensive critical notes.

MARY SCOTT HARRISON MCKEE (April 3, 1858–October 28, 1930) was the only daughter of President Benjamin Harrison and his first wife, Caroline Scott Harrison. When her mother died on October 25, 1892, two weeks before the election that turned her father out of office, Mary took over as White House hostess for the final four months of his term.

In November 1884, Mary married James Robert McKee (1857–1942), and after her father was elected President, she, her husband, and their two children lived with her parents in the White House through his term.

After retiring from the Presidency, Harrison became romantically involved with his late wife's niece, widow Mary Lord Dimmick, who was 27 days younger than his own daughter. His two now-grown children were opposed to the relationship, and neither Mary McKee nor her brother attended their wedding in 1896. Indeed Mary McKee never spoke to her father again. She returned to Indianapolis during his final illness in March 1901, but arrived several hours after his death.

MARGARET WOODROW WILSON (April 16, 1886–February 12, 1944) was the eldest of President Woodrow Wilson's three daughters (and the only one to not marry). After her mother's death (August 6, 1914), she served as White House hostess until her father met and then married Edith Bolling Galt (December 18, 1915).

Margaret sang and made several recordings around 1918. About 1940 she traveled to the ashram of Sri Aurobindo in Pondicherry, French India (also known as Puducherry, India), where she chose to stay for the rest of her life. While there, she was known as "Nistha," the Sanskrit word for sincerity. She and scholar Joseph Campbell edited the English translation of *The Gospel of Sri Ramakrishna* by Swami Nikhilananda, which was published in 1942.

In her father's last will, he left her an annuity of $2,500, as long as that amount did not exceed one-third of the annual income of his estate.

31. First Ladies' Causes and Projects

Before the adoption of the 19th Amendment—which guaranteed women the right to vote—in 1920, First Ladies didn't play major roles beyond being adjuncts of their husbands; they were usually the official White House hostesses, but rarely considered in their own right, other than perhaps as fashion icons. The early First Ladies are rarely remembered except as the wives of Presidents, with a few exceptions:

JAMES MADISON'S wife, DOLLEY (1809–17), is remembered for rescuing George Washington's portrait before the British arrived to burn the White House during the War of 1812.

RUTHERFORD HAYES'S wife, LUCY (1877–81), was known for keeping alcohol out of the White House and, along with her husband, hosted the first official Easter egg roll on the White House grounds in 1878.

BENJAMIN HARRISON'S first wife, CAROLINE (1889–92), as First Lady, helped found the Daughters of the American Revolution and served as the society's first President General.

As the women's suffrage movement gained steam, First Ladies looked beyond the walls of the White House. WOODROW WILSON'S first wife, ELLEN (1913–14), worked to improve housing in Washington's Negro slums, by visiting the neighborhoods and bringing the attention of Congress. One of her dying wishes was that the alley-clearance bill, then still pending in Congress, would pass. Two days after her death, it was adopted.

After Ellen's death, WOODROW WILSON married EDITH in late 1915. The expansion of World War I, and then US entry into the war, left little time for other projects, but Edith did show leadership as a war wife: her White

House followed national rationing days, and she brought in a flock of sheep to graze on the White House lawns, freeing up the manpower such tasks ordinarily required. She accompanied Woodrow on his extended trip to Europe at the conclusion of the war, during which time he helped create the League of Nations, and accompanied him on his trip around the country to campaign for it when they returned. Following his stroke in 1919, Edith cared for Woodrow, and though she later claimed that she only reviewed documents for him to judge their importance, there is some thought that she was actually making decisions in his stead, as she would let no one other than his medical team in to see him.

The 19th Amendment became law in the summer of 1920, and Warren Harding was the first President elected with the women's vote. On March 4, 1921, FLORENCE HARDING became First Lady (1921–23) and took a much more politically active role than her predecessors. She influenced Warren's selection of Cabinet members and publically made her views known on a wide range of topics. The cause she championed above all others was the welfare of war veterans.

Before she met CALVIN COOLIDGE, GRACE (1923–29) studied lip reading at the Clarke Schools for Hearing and Speech and then became a teacher there. Teaching the deaf became her lifelong passion, and after Calvin's death, she continued to work on behalf of the deaf.

LOU HOOVER (1929–33) became the first First Lady to broadcast on the radio on a regular basis. She did not have her own radio program, but frequently appeared as a guest speaker, often advocating for volunteerism or discussing the work of the Girl Scouts. Before becoming First Lady, she had served as the National President of the Girl Scouts of the USA (1922–25), and then she took up the post again after they left the White House (1935–37). Camp Lou Henry Hoover in Middleville, New Jersey, is named for her.

The mold of the demure First Lady who was seen but not heard was already cracking, and when ELEANOR ROOSEVELT (1933–45) became First Lady, she destroyed that mold. In 1921, following the onset of Franklin's polio, Eleanor began serving as his stand-in, making public appearances for him, and while he was Governor of New York, she traveled widely in the state, making speeches and inspecting state facilities on his behalf, and then reporting her findings to him at the end of each trip. She also involved herself in labor rights movements and in Democratic Party politics.

When Franklin took office as President, she maintained her personal activities and continued lecturing for large fees (by 1941, she was earning $1,000 per lecture; at the time, the President's salary was $75,000 a year). She also continued in her now-accustomed role of traveling on his behalf. She was the first Presidential spouse to hold a press conference (she went on to hold 348 press conferences during her 12 years in the White House). And as part of her civil-rights activism, she banned male reporters from her press conferences, forcing newspapers to keep female reporters on staff in order to cover them. In 1940, she became the first Presidential spouse to speak at a national-party convention.

One of her earliest projects as First Lady was the development of Arthurdale, a planned community to house miners who had been black-listed for union activities in West Virginia: she agitated for Congressional support for the project and personally funded portions of it. She was also a very active civil-rights proponent for African-Americans and for women. And when the United States entered World War II, she spoke out against anti-Japanese prejudice and privately opposed her husband's Executive Order 9066, which forced Japanese-Americans into internment camps.

During the war, she worked to allow more refugees into the United States and co-chaired the Office of Civilian Defense, which was a federal emergency-war agency set up to coordinate state and federal measures for protection of civilians in case of war emergency. She also made several overseas trips to visit the troops, both to improve their morale and give her husband firsthand reports.

Her syndicated newspaper column, "My Day," appeared six days a week from 1935 to 1962. In it, she wrote about the events in her days, about causes she supported (such as civil rights, women's rights, and labor rights), and about news events of major import. That column may have been the most visible platform of any First Lady.

Eight months after Franklin's death, President Truman appointed Eleanor a delegate to the United Nations General Assembly, and she was the first chairperson of the United Nations Commission on Human Rights (1946–51). She played an instrumental role in drafting the Universal Declaration of Human Rights and also served as the US Representative to the Commission. In 1968, the UN posthumously awarded her one of its first Human Rights Prizes.

In 1961, President Kennedy named her Chair of the Presidential Commission on the Status of Women. She died just before the commission issued its report.

BESS TRUMAN (1945–53) and MAMIE EISENHOWER (1953–61) were less interested in taking such active roles. Bess spent much of her time as First Lady at home in Missouri, only returning to Washington during the social season, and in her nearly eight years as First Lady, she had only one press conference, for which the questions had to be submitted ahead of time in writing. Mamie, too, was much more the supportive wife and social hostess than an instrument for societal change.

But then came JACQUELINE KENNEDY (1961–63). One of the youngest First Ladies, she made redecorating and restoring the White House a very public project. Earlier First Ladies had had a hand in choosing furnishings and changing the decor, but Jacqueline Kennedy was the first to see the Executive Mansion as a museum, a connection to the history of the country. Her pre-inauguration tour of the building disappointed her, as she found very little historic significance in the house and its undistinguished furnishings. When the Kennedys moved in, she set out to make the family quarters attractive and suitable for family life, and almost immediately ran out of funds. So she established a fine-arts committee to oversee and fund the restoration process. She initiated publication of the first White House guidebook, the sales of which funded the restoration; she promoted a Congressional bill that made the White House furnishings the property of the Smithsonian Institution, rather than available to departing ex-Presidents to claim as their own; and she worked to have pieces of historical interest donated to the White House. On February 14, 1962, she hosted a televised tour of the White House which won a special Emmy Award. Her restoration and preservation efforts resulted in the formation of the White House Historical Association, the Committee for the Preservation of the White House, a permanent Curator of the White House, the White House Endowment Trust, and the White House Acquisition Trust. In her retirement—after the death of her second husband, Aristotle Onassis—she returned to her preservation work, spearheading a campaign to save and renovate New York City's Grand Central Terminal.

After Jacqueline Kennedy beautified the inside of the White House, LADY BIRD JOHNSON (1963–69) expanded those efforts outside the building. She started a capital beautification project, known as the "Society for a More Beautiful National Capital," to improve physical conditions in Washington, DC, by planting millions of flowers. Her efforts were guided by her statement "where flowers bloom, so does hope." She worked extensively with the American Association of Nurserymen to protect wildflowers and plant them along highways. To that end, she was instrumental in promoting the Highway Beautification Act, which was nicknamed "Lady Bird's Bill." After Lyndon's death, she served on the board of regents for the University of Texas, on the National Park Service Advisory Board, and on National Geographic's Board of Trustees. In 1982, along with actress Helen Hayes, she founded the National Wildflower Research Center, a nonprofit organization devoted to preserving and reintroducing native plants in planned landscapes. Lady Bird was also a staunch advocate of the Head Start program, and during the 1964 Presidential election, she campaigned on her own for her husband and to promote the Civil Rights Act.

PAT NIXON'S (1969–74) choice of projects was less showy but no less impactful: she promoted the concept of volunteerism, encouraging people to address social problems at the local level through volunteering at hospitals, civic organizations, and rehabilitation centers. She said, "Our success as a nation depends on our willingness to give generously of ourselves for the welfare and enrichment of the lives of others." Leading by example, she belonged to several volunteer groups, including Women in Community Services and the Urban Services League, and she was an advocate of the Domestic Volunteer Service Act of 1973. She was also involved in the development of recreation areas and park land, was a member of the President's Committee on Employment of the Handicapped, and lent her support to organizations dedicated to improving the lives of handicapped children.

In the White House, she continued Jacqueline Kennedy's efforts to turn the building into a museum, adding more than 600 paintings and furnishings to the collections (the largest number of acquisitions by any single Administration). She created the Map Room, renovated the China Room, refurbished nine others, and directed the development of the White House's exterior-lighting system.

In personal and political relations, Pat spoke in favor of women running for political office and encouraged her husband to nominate a woman to the Supreme Court, saying "woman power is unbeatable; I've seen it all across this country." She was the first First Lady to publicly support the Equal Rights Amendment and, in 1972, became the second First Lady to address a national-party nominating convention.

BETTY FORD (1974–77) became an advocate for health in many aspects. She was outspoken about formerly taboo topics, including marijuana use and premarital sex, and openly talked about her battle with breast cancer (she underwent a mastectomy on September 28, 1974, less than two months after becoming First Lady). She said she'd decided to discuss it publicly because: "There had been so much cover-up during Watergate that we wanted to be sure there would be no cover-up in the Ford Administration." But she also told *Time* magazine, "When other women have this same operation, it doesn't make any headlines. But the fact that I was the wife of the President put it in headlines and brought before the public this particular experience I was going through. It made a lot of women realize that it could happen to them. I'm sure I've saved at least one person—maybe more." Several weeks after Ford's operation, Second Lady Happy Rockefeller also had a mastectomy, and the spike in women self-examining after their public discussions led to an increase in reported cases of breast cancer, which was known as the "Betty Ford blip." After the Fords left the White House, Betty admitted her alcoholism and addiction to pain killers, and went into treatment for substance abuse. After her recovery, she established the Betty Ford Center for the treatment of chemical dependency. She chaired the center's board of directors until 2005, when her daughter, Susan, took over. In 1987, she co-wrote a book about her treatment: *Betty: A Glad Awakening*, and in 2003, she wrote *Healing and Hope: Six Women from the Betty Ford Center Share Their Powerful Journeys of Addiction and Recovery*.

When JIMMY CARTER took office, ROSALYNN (1977–81) announced that she had no intention of being a traditional First Lady and instead involved herself in West Wing policy. She sat in on Cabinet meetings (at her husband's invitation), frequently represented him at ceremonial occasions, and served as his personal emissary to Latin American countries. She became the honorary chairperson of the international cultural-exchange program Friendship Force International when it debuted in March 1977 (she held that position until 2002). In 1977, she joined her predecessors Lady Bird Johnson and Betty Ford in campaigning for the Equal Rights Amendment at the Houston conference celebrating the International Women's Year. She also served as an active honorary chair of the President's Commission on Mental Health. On behalf of the Mental Health System Bill of 1980, she testified before a Senate committee, becoming the second First Lady to appear before the Congress (after Eleanor Roosevelt). After leaving the White House, the Carters jointly founded The Carter Center, which works to advance human rights and alleviate human suffering. She is still a member of the Center's Board of Trustees and focuses on mental-health programs.

In her first year, NANCY REAGAN (1981–89) directed a major renovation of the White House, but publicly stumbled when her attempts to bring elegance back to the Executive Mansion through conspicuous consumption earned her criticism for being out of touch with a country suffering economic difficulties. In 1982, she launched her "Just Say No" drug-awareness campaign, which was her major project for the rest of her time as First Lady. The campaign focused on drug education and teaching young people of the dangers of drug abuse. After Ronald's reelection, she expanded the campaign to an international level and, in 1988, became the first First Lady invited to address the United Nations General Assembly, where she spoke on international drug-interdiction and trafficking laws.

BARBARA BUSH'S (1989–93) cause as First Lady (a carryover from her eight years as Second Lady) was family literacy: she called it "the most important issue we have." She helped develop the Barbara Bush Foundation for Family Literacy (she chaired the foundation until 2012; her daughter Doro is the current honorary chair) and is dedicated to eliminating the generational cycle of illiteracy in America by supporting programs where parents and their young children are able to learn together. She spoke regularly on *Mrs. Bush's Story Time*, a national radio program that stressed the importance of reading aloud to children. She also wrote the 1992 bestseller *Millie's Book: As Dictated to Barbara Bush* (credited to her dog) about Millie's new litter of puppies. Some critics note that she was more popular than the First Ladies who preceded and succeeded her—Nancy Reagan and Hillary Clinton—because she avoided controversy and took very few public positions on political issues.

Referring to his wife's abilities and experience during his Presidential campaign, Bill Clinton offered the voters "two for the price of one," but that gambit earned more derision than praise. Nevertheless, after he took office, HILLARY CLINTON (1993–2001; she was the first First Lady to hold a postgraduate degree—she earned her JD from Yale in 1973—and was a practicing lawyer until she moved into the White House) was the first First Lady to have an office in the West Wing (in addition to the usual First Lady offices in the East Wing). She played a major role in the new Administration, vetting appointments and contributing to policy decisions. As First Lady, Hillary Clinton was one of the two most publicly empowered Presidential wives (along with Eleanor Roosevelt). Critics said it was inappropriate for the First Lady to have such a major role in matters of public policy; supporters noted it was no different than other White House advisors and that voters had been well aware that she would play such an active role.

In January 1993, Bill appointed Hillary to chair the Task Force on National Health Care Reform (echoing her successful efforts as First Lady of Arkansas in the field of education reform). The task force's recommendation, known positively as the Clinton health-care plan and negatively as "Hillarycare," was a comprehensive proposal that would require employers to provide health coverage to their employees through individual health-maintenance organizations. The proposal failed to get enough support in the Congress (even though the Clintons' Democratic Party controlled both houses) and was finally abandoned in September 1994. Following the Democrats' dismal showing in the 1994 midterm elections, the White House tried to downplay Hillary's role in shaping policy. Nevertheless, she was a major force behind the adoption of the 1997 State Children's Health Insurance Program—a federal effort that provided state support for children whose parents could not provide them with health coverage—and participated in outreach efforts to enroll children in the program once it became law. She promoted nationwide immunization against childhood illnesses and encouraged older women to have mammograms to detect breast cancer, with coverage provided by Medicare.

In concert with Attorney General Janet Reno, she helped create the Office on Violence Against Women at the Department of Justice and, in 1997, spearheaded the Adoption and Safe Families Act.

She was the Founding Chair of the Save America's Treasures program, a national effort that matched federal funds to private donations to preserve and restore historic items and sites, including the flag that inspired "The Star-Spangled Banner" and the First Ladies Historic Site in Canton, Ohio. She also created the first White House Sculpture Garden, located in the Jacqueline Kennedy Garden, which displayed large contemporary American works of art loaned from museums.

Near the end of the Clintons' White House years, Hillary broke with all tradition by running for and winning election to the Senate while she was still First Lady, setting up a residence in New York state to run for the seat being vacated by Daniel Patrick Moynihan. Her post-White House political career (eight years in the Senate, four years as Secretary of State, and a strong contender for the Democratic nomination for President in both 2008 and 2016), in retrospect, tinges her efforts as First Lady with the appearance of simply laying the groundwork for her grander plans for the future.

LAURA BUSH (2001–09), who has an MS in Library Science, was a librarian before the rise of her husband's political star and, as First Lady, championed the cause of education. She worked to recruit highly qualified teachers to ensure that young children would be taught well, and she focused on early child development. In 2001, she partnered with the Library of Congress to launch the annual National Book Festival, and in 2002, she testified before the Senate Committee on Education, asking for higher teachers' salaries and better training for Head Start programs. She also created a national initiative called "Ready to Read, Ready to Learn," which promotes reading at a young age. The United Nations named her honorary ambassador for the UN Decade of Literacy, and in that post, she hosted a Conference on Global Literacy in 2006. In 2008, Laura co-authored a children's book with her daughter, Jenna, called *Read All About It!*

She also focused on the health and wellbeing of women. She established the Women's Health and Wellness Initiative, and became involved with The Heart Truth (a campaign to raise awareness about heart disease in women and how to prevent the condition).

MICHELLE OBAMA (2009–) is the second First Lady with a law degree (hers is from Harvard), and while she did make appearances to support her husband's policy initiatives in the first months of his Presidency, she has been a far less polarizing figure than Hillary Clinton was before her. Michelle extended the efforts of her predecessors toward healthy eating in the White House by planting the organic White House Kitchen Garden and installing bee hives on the South Lawn. In early 2010, she announced the program she hoped would be her legacy: "Let's Move!" The project is an attempt to reverse the twenty-first-century trend toward childhood obesity and, in concert with Barack's Task Force on Childhood Obesity, aims to create a national plan toward change. Her 2012 book *American Grown: The Story of the White House Kitchen Garden and Gardens Across America* is based on her experiences with the garden and promotes healthy eating.

THE FIRST LADIES: HOME AND FAMILY

32. The First Ladies Who Had the Most Children

The 48 women who were married to the Presidents produced 164 children—94 boys and 70 girls—of whom 125 lived to adulthood. These numbers do not include stepchildren, adopted children, or Warren Harding's illegitimate daughter by Nan Britton, but they do include Martha Washington's four children with her first husband, Daniel Parke Custis; Dolley Madison's two children with her first husband, John Todd; and Florence Harding's son by her first husband, Henry De Wolfe.

1. ANNA SYMMES TUTHILL (1775–1864) married William Henry Harrison in 1795, and they had 10 children in the next 19 years. Four of those children survived to see their father become President in 1841, and one of them fathered a President himself (though neither he nor his parents lived to see Benjamin Harrison inaugurated). The children were: Elizabeth Bassett (1796–1846); John Cleves Symmes (1798–1830); Lucy Singleton (1800–26); William Henry, Jr. (1802–38); John Scott (1804–78; he served in the House of Representatives 1853–57,

and was the father of President Benjamin Harrison); Benjamin (1806–40); Mary Symmes (1809–42); Carter Bassett (1811–39); Anna Tuthill (1813–65); and James Findlay (1814–19). They combined to give Anna and William 48 grandchildren.

2 (tie). LETITIA CHRISTIAN (1790–1842) married John Tyler in 1813, and they had eight children between 1815 and 1830. Seven of the children lived long enough to see their father elected Vice President and succeed to the Presidency upon William Henry Harrison's death, in 1841. The children were: Mary (1815–48); Robert (1816–77); John (1819–96); Letitia (1821–1907); Elizabeth "Lizzie" (1823–50); Anne Contesse (1825–25); Alice (1827–54); and Tazewell (1830–74). They combined to give Letitia and John 24 grandchildren.

2 (tie). LUCY WARE WEBB (1831–89) married Rutherford Hayes in 1852, and they had eight children in the next 22 years. Five of the children lived long enough to see their father become President in 1877. The children were: Sardis Birchard, aka Birchard Austin (1853–1926); James Webb, aka Webb Cook (1856–1935); Rutherford Platt (1858–1927); Joseph Thompson (1861–63); George Crook (1864–66); Frances "Fanny" (1867–1950); Scott Russell (1871–1923); and Manning Force (1873–74). The Hayes children gave their parents a relatively scant nine grandchildren.

4 (tie). MARTHA WAYLES (1748–82) married her first husband, Bathurst Skelton, in 1766, when she was 18. Their son, John, was born in 1767, and Bathurst died in 1768. John died in 1771, and on New Year's Day, 1772, Martha married Thomas Jefferson. They had six children (five girls and one boy) between 1772 and 1782, but only two of them—oldest daughter Martha "Patsy" and fourth daughter Mary "Maria"—lived to adulthood. Martha died 19 years before Thomas became President. Patsy (1772–1836) had 12 children, 10 of whom lived to adulthood, giving Martha and Thomas 30 great-grandchildren. Maria (1778–1804) had three children

of whom only one lived to adulthood, but that one, Francis Eppes, gave Martha and Thomas 13 great-grandchildren.

4 (tie). JULIA GARDINER (1820–89) married President John Tyler in 1844, 21 months after the death of his first wife (see above). After he retired from the Presidency, they had seven children: (David) Gardiner (1846–1927); John Alexander (1848–83); Julia Gardiner (1849–71); Lachlan (1851–1902); Lyon Gardiner (1853–1935); Robert FitzWalter (1856–1927); and Pearl (1860–1947). They combined to give Julia and John 23 grandchildren. Thus, John Tyler's 15 children gave him 47 grandchildren. Two of Lyon's sons with his second wife, Sue Ruffin, are still living at this writing (Lyon Gardiner Tyler, Jr., born in 1924, and Harrison Ruffin Tyler, born in 1928), making John Tyler the earliest former President of the United States with living grandchildren.

4 (tie). LUCRETIA RUDOLPH (1832–1918) married James Garfield in 1858. They had seven children, five of whom lived to see their father's Presidency (1881). The children were: Eliza Arabella (1860–63); Harry Augustus (1863–1942); James Rudolf (1865–1950; he was Secretary of the Interior from 1907 to 1909); Mary (1867–1947); Irvin McDowell (1870–1951); Abram (1872–1958); and Edward (1874–76). They combined to give Lucretia and James 13 grandchildren.

33. The First Ladies Who Had the Fewest Children

The 48 women who were married to the Presidents combined to bear 164 children—94 boys and 70 girls—of whom 125 lived to adulthood. The average number of children is nearly four, but the five women who had the most combined to produce 40 children. Four of the First Ladies had no children:

RACHEL DONELSON ROBARDS (1767–1828) married Andrew Jackson in 1794. They had no children, but they did adopt her brother's son in 1810, and named him Andrew Jackson, Jr.

SARAH CHILDRESS (1803–91) married James Knox Polk in 1824. They had no children in their 25 years of marriage (he died months after retiring from the Presidency).

CAROLINE CARMICHAEL MCINTOSH (1813–81) married former President Millard Fillmore in 1858. They were both widowed and had no children together (though he did have two children with his first wife).

EDITH BOLLING (1872–1961) married Norman Galt in 1896. He died in 1908, without fathering any children. She met and married the recently widowed President Woodrow Wilson in 1915. They, too, had no children (though he did have three children with his first wife).

Three Presidential wives had children, but not with their President-husbands:

MARTHA DANDRIDGE (1731–1802) married Daniel Parke Custis about 1750, and they had four children before he died in 1757 (two of the children predeceased their father). She then married George Washington in 1759.

DOLLEY PAYNE (1768–1849) married John Todd, Jr., and had two children with him, in 1792 and 1793. He and their second son died in 1793, and she married James Madison in 1794.

FLORENCE MABEL KLING (1860–1924) married Henry De Wolfe in 1880, six months before their son was born. She divorced him in 1886 and married Warren Harding in 1891.

Four other Presidential wives had one child each with their President-husbands:

MARY SCOTT LORD DIMMICK (1858–1948) married President Benjamin Harrison in 1896, three years after he retired from the Presidency and three and a half years after the death of his first wife, her aunt. They had one child, Elizabeth (1897–1955).

ALICE HATHAWAY LEE (1861–84) married Theodore Roosevelt in 1880. They had one daughter, who was named for the mother, two days before she died on February 14, 1884: Alice Lee Roosevelt (1884–1980). In 1886, Theodore married his second wife, Edith Kermit Carow. He became President 17 years after his first wife's death.

ELIZABETH VIRGINIA "BESS" WALLACE (1885–1982) married Harry Truman in 1919. They had one daughter: (Mary) Margaret (1924–2008).

HILLARY DIANE RODHAM (1947–) married Bill Clinton in 1975. They have one daughter: Chelsea Victoria, who was born in 1980.

34. The Five First Ladies Who Outlived Their Husbands by the Longest Time

The Presidents are, on average, four and a quarter years older than their 42 first wives, and 16 and a half years older than their six second wives, so it only makes sense that the First Ladies will outlive their President-husbands by some length of time. The actual numbers, however, may be surprising. Of the 36 sets of first wives and Presidents who are both deceased, the wives outlived their husbands by an average of two years, 313 days. Of the five sets of second wives and Presidents who are both deceased, the wives outlived their husbands by an average of 29 years, 318 days.

1. MARY SCOTT LORD DIMMICK HARRISON: 46 years, 298 days. The second wife of Benjamin Harrison (1885–89) was born on April 30, 1858, nearly 25 years after her husband. Mary was Harrison's first wife's niece and was widowed soon after her first marriage. In 1889, she moved into the White House to serve as her aunt's assistant. First Lady Caroline Harrison died in 1892, and the widowed now ex-President and his niece soon fell in love. His two grown children (both of whom were older than their new stepmother) did not approve and did not attend the wedding, which took place on April 6, 1896. Mary and Benjamin had a daughter in 1897. Harrison died on March 13, 1901, aged 67. Mary died on January 5, 1948, three months before her 90th birthday.

2. SARAH CHILDRESS POLK: 42 years, 60 days. Born on September 4, 1803, the future First Lady was 20 when she married the 28-year-old James Knox Polk on January 1, 1824. After his one term as President (1845–49), the Polks retired to their newly purchased home in Nashville, Tennessee. James died three months after leaving office, at the age of 53, the youngest President to die after leaving office and the President who had the shortest

retirement from office. Sarah, however, was much longer lived than her husband. She died on August 14, 1891, at the age of 87, and was buried next to her husband at their home. Later, they were both reinterred at the state capitol.

3. FRANCES FOLSOM CLEVELAND: 39 years, 127 days. Frances was the daughter of Oscar Folsom, Grover Cleveland's law partner. She was born on July 21, 1864. Upon her father's death in 1875, Cleveland became her guardian. While she was in college, he developed romantic feelings for her, and he proposed in August 1885, soon after she graduated. They were married on June 2, 1886, in the Blue Room of the White House, and Frances—aged 21—became the youngest First Lady ever. The first of their five children, Ruth, was born in 1891, between Cleveland's two terms. In 1892, he was reelected, and he served to 1897. Esther, in 1893, became the only child of a President to be born in the White House. The former President died on June 24, 1908, aged 71. Frances, who was 27 years younger, became the first Presidential widow to remarry, in 1913, when she married Thomas J. Preston, a professor of archeology at Princeton University. She died on October 29, 1947, and was buried next to Cleveland in Princeton, New Jersey.

4. EDITH BOLLING GALT WILSON: 37 years, 328 days. President Woodrow Wilson's first wife, Ellen, died during his first term of office, on August 6, 1914. In March 1915, the President's cousin, Helen Bones, introduced Edith—herself a widow—to Woodrow. He proposed in May (although the engagement was kept a secret until October). When they married on December 18, 1915, he was 58, she was 43 (she was born on October 15, 1872). Following the President's stroke in September 1919, Edith guarded him and kept anyone from seeing him. There is some evidence to suggest that she wasn't merely helping Woodrow, but was actually acting as President in his stead. Following Wilson's retirement, they lived in Washington, DC, where she nursed him until his death on February 3, 1924. Edith remained active in the capital's social scene and attended

President John Kennedy's inauguration in 1961. She died on December 28, 1961, at the age of 89.

5. LUCRETIA RUDOLPH GARFIELD: 36 years, 166 days. Lucretia "Crete" was born on April 19, 1832, five months after her future husband, James Abram Garfield. They were married on November 11, 1858, and had five children between 1863 and 1872. As First Lady, Lucretia planned to research the history of the White House, aiming to restore it, but she contracted malaria. James was on his way to visit her in New Jersey when he was shot in July 1881. He died in September, and she moved to England to live in anonymity, but eventually returned to their home in Ohio. She lived on a trust fund financier Cyrus W. Field had raised for her and her children, and spent her winters in South Pasadena, California, where on March 14, 1918, she died a month before her 86th birthday.

If we factor out Harrison and Wilson, who were their husbands' second wives, CLAUDIA ALTA "LADY BIRD" TAYLOR JOHNSON would be fourth on the list. Lady Bird, born December 22, 1912, was four years younger than Lyndon Baines Johnson when they married on November 17, 1934. She became First Lady when President Kennedy was assassinated and was standing next to her husband, the Vice President, when he took the oath of office aboard Air Force 1 in Dallas, Texas, in November 1963. Following his own term in office, they retired to their ranch in Texas. As First Lady, and after Lyndon's death on January 22, 1973, she spearheaded a program of beautification and wildflower conservation and, in later years, was known as one of the founders of the environmental movement. She died on July 11, 2007, aged 94. She was the second longest-lived First Lady and outlived her husband by 34 years, 170 days.

Fifth on the list would be JACQUELINE LEE BOUVIER KENNEDY ONASSIS. She was born on July 28, 1929, and married the future President John Fitzgerald Kennedy on September 12, 1953 (she was 24; he was 36). As First Lady, she redecorated the White House to return it to its former glory, led a televised tour of the building, and was a patron of the arts. She was with her husband when he was assassinated in Dallas, Texas, on November 22, 1963. In 1968, she married Aristotle Onassis, a Greek shipping tycoon. He died in 1975. Following his death, she became an editor for Doubleday and lived a very private life. She died on May 19, 1994, two months before her 65th birthday and 30 years, 178 days after her President-husband. She was buried next to him in Arlington National Cemetery.

35. The Five First Ladies Who Predeceased Their Husbands by the Longest Time

1. MARTHA JEFFERSON. After 10 years of marriage, Martha died on September 6, 1782, four months after giving birth to her sixth child. She was a month shy of her 34th birthday. Thomas never remarried. He was elected President in 1801, reelected in 1805, and died on the 50th anniversary of the Declaration of Independence he'd written during their marriage: July 4, 1826. Martha had predeceased him by 43 years, 301 days.

2. HANNAH VAN BUREN. Hannah died of tuberculosis on February 5, 1819, 16 days before her 12th wedding anniversary and a month before her 36th birthday. Martin never remarried, but was elected President 17 years later (after serving one term as Vice President). He lost his bid for reelection and died on July 24, 1862: 43 years, 169 days after his wife.

3. ALICE ROOSEVELT. Alice died at the age of 22, from a combination of Bright's disease and complications from childbirth, on February 14, 1880 (her daughter, Alice, had been born two days before). Her husband, Theodore, was grief-stricken, both because of her death and that of his mother (she died on the same day). In 1886, he married Edith Carow, a friend who had attended his and Alice's wedding, and was President from 1901 to 1909. He died January 6, 1919: 34 years, 326 days after Alice (and nearly 30 years before Edith).

4. ABIGAIL FILLMORE. The first First Lady on this list to have lived through her husband's Presidency, Abigail died of pneumonia she caught during

Franklin Pierce's inaugural festivities. She survived husband Millard's term by 26 days, dying on March 30, 1853. Millard married widow Caroline Carmichael McIntosh in 1858 and then died on March 8, 1874. Abigail predeceased him by 20 years, 343 days (Caroline died in 1881).

5. LOU HOOVER. She married Herbert on February 10, 1899, two months before her 25th birthday and six months before his. In 1928, he was elected President; in 1933, he retired from the Presidency. Lou died on January 7, 1944, but Herbert survived until October 20, 1964. Lou predeceased him by 20 years, 257 days.

36. The Most Married First Ladies (Those Who Were Married More Than Once)

Of the 43 Presidents, six were married twice, one not at all, and the rest once each. Of the 48 women who were married to Presidents, 36 were married only once.

Six Presidential wives were widowed before marrying their President-husbands:

1. MARTHA WASHINGTON (1731–1802) married 39-year-old Daniel Parke Custis in 1750, when she was 19. They had four children, two of whom died young, before his death in 1757. A year and a half later, she married George Washington and was the first First Lady (although the term hadn't yet been coined) from 1789 to 1797. He died in 1799, and she in 1802.

2. MARTHA JEFFERSON (1748–82) married Bathurst Skelton (1744–68) in 1766. They had one son (who died in 1771). On January 1, 1772, she married Thomas Jefferson, with whom she had six children (two of whom lived to adulthood). She died more than 18 years before her husband became the third President.

3. DOLLEY MADISON (1768–1849) married John Todd (1764–93) in 1790. They had two sons (John Payne Todd, who lived to the age of 60, and one who died an infant) during their short marriage. In 1794, she married James Madison and assisted with White House hostessing duties for Thomas Jefferson (while her husband was Secretary of State) before becoming First Lady when her husband was elected President.

4. CAROLINE FILLMORE (1813–81) was the first woman to marry a former President. In 1832, she married Ezekiel C. McIntosh (1806–55), who left

her a wealthy widow when he died. In 1858, she married Millard Fillmore, who had retired from the Presidency (and then been widowed himself) five years earlier. They were together for 16 years, until his death.

5. MARY HARRISON (1858–1948) married Walter Erskine Dimmick (1856–82) in 1881. He died a few months after they were married. She lived in the White House while her aunt, Caroline Harrison, was First Lady, helping with the hostessing duties. Caroline died a few weeks before her husband, Benjamin Harrison, lost his bid for reelection. In 1896, Mary married Benjamin (to the consternation of his two grown children). They had a daughter the next year, and then he died in 1901. Mary survived another 47 years.

6. EDITH WILSON (1872–1961) married Norman Galt in 1896. He died in 1908. Soon after Woodrow Wilson's first wife, Ellen, died in 1914 (while he was President), he was introduced to Edith. They married in 1915. After retiring from the White House, she nursed him for another three years, until his death in 1924. Edith remained active in Washington and outlived her President-husband by 37 years. She attended John Kennedy's inauguration in 1961 and died in December of that year. The day of her death, which would have been Woodrow's 105th birthday, she was scheduled to be the guest of honor at the dedication of the Woodrow Wilson Bridge.

Four Presidential wives were divorced before marrying their President-husbands (only one President, Ronald Reagan, had been divorced):

1. RACHEL JACKSON (1767–1828) married Lewis Robards in 1785, but it didn't work out. They separated in 1790, and she returned to her parents' home. She thought they were divorced and married Andrew Jackson in 1791. But then Robards returned, claiming they were still married (thus invalidating her marriage to Jackson). Their official divorce was finalized in at the beginning of 1794, and she remarried Jackson on January 17 of that year. That claimed bigamy was an issue in the election of 1828, but Jackson

overcame the mutterings and was elected. Rachel died December 22, 1828, after her husband was elected President, but before he was inaugurated.

2. FLORENCE HARDING (1860–1924) is assumed to have married Henry "Pete" Athenton DeWolfe in 1880, although no marriage license has ever been found, so it may have been a common law marriage. At any rate, they had one son and then divorced in 1886 (he died in the 1890s). In 1891, she married Warren Harding, who was five years younger than she. They remained married until he died in office in 1923.

3. BETTY FORD (1918–2011) married William C. Warren in 1942, but the marriage didn't work out, and they divorced in September 1947. In October 1948, she married Gerald Ford, with whom she had four children. They were married for 58 years, until his death in December 2006 (nearly 30 years after he retired from the Presidency).

4. JANE WYMAN (1917–2007) was born Sarah Jane Faulks and was an actress. She is assumed to have married Ernest Eugene Wyman (1906–70) in 1933, but there is no documentary proof of the marriage (and her stage name may have been taken from her mother). It is known, however, that she married Myron Martin Futterman (1900–65) in June 1937. They separated in October of that year and officially divorced in December 1938. In 1940, she married actor Ronald Reagan (1911–2004), who was elected President in 1980. The Reagans had two children and adopted one more, before their divorce in 1949. On November 1, 1952, Jane married Fred Karger (1916–79), but divorced him on December 30, 1955. She remarried Karger on March 11, 1961, and divorced him again on March 9, 1965. She remained unmarried for the rest of her life.

And two Presidential widows remarried after the deaths of their President-husbands:

1. FRANCES CLEVELAND (1864–1947) was the youngest First Lady ever when she married President Grover Cleveland two months before her 22nd

birthday (he was 49 at the time). They had five children between 1891 and 1903, before his death in 1908. In February 1913, she became the first Presidential widow to remarry, when she married Princeton professor Thomas Jex Preston, Jr. (1862–1955). After her death, she was buried with her first husband, the President.

2. JACQUELINE KENNEDY (1929–94) married John Kennedy in 1953 (he was 12 years older than she) and had four children between 1956 and 1963 (two lived to adulthood). She had just recovered from the death of her fourth child and started making public appearances again when her husband was assassinated in November 1963. In October 1968, she married Greek shipping tycoon Aristotle Onassis (1906–75) as his second or third wife (reports of his potential first marriage vary). After Onassis's death, she lived in New York City and worked as an editor. After her death, she was buried with her President-husband in Arlington National Cemetery.

37. The Women Who Married Presidents to Become First Lady

1. JULIA GARDINER was born on July 23, 1820, 30 years after her future husband, and raised on Long Island, New York. In early 1842, she met President John Tyler at a White House reception. On September 10, 1842, Tyler's wife, Letitia, died after suffering a stroke. Julia and Tyler began seeing each other in 1843. He proposed, only to be turned down, but she eventually said yes. On February 28, 1844, President Tyler and several others were aboard the USS *Princeton*, an advanced warship, for an inspection. An explosion killed the Secretaries of State and the Navy; Julia's father, David Gardiner; and several others. In the wake of this tragedy, Tyler and Julia decided on a low-key wedding, and on June 26, 1844, Reverend Benjamin T. Onderdonk married them at the Church of the Ascension in New York City. Julia's sister and brother were the bridesmaid and best man. Tyler's son, John Tyler, Jr., was the only one of his seven surviving children to attend and the only one to know about the wedding. Tyler's sons readily accepted Julia into the family. His daughters, however, were less happy (especially his eldest daughter, Mary, who was five years older than her new stepmother). After post-wedding trips to Philadelphia and Tyler's home in Virginia, they returned to the White House, where Julia served as First Lady for the final few months of her husband's term.

2. FRANCES FOLSOM was born on July 21, 1864, to Oscar and Emma Harmon Folsom. Her father was a lawyer whose partner and close friend was 27-year-old Grover Cleveland. When Oscar died in 1875, without a will, Cleveland was appointed administrator of his estate. While Frances was in Wells College, Cleveland's feelings for her became more romantic than paternal. In 1884, Cleveland was elected President. Frances graduated from college in 1885, and he proposed by letter that August. She

accepted, but they didn't announce their engagement until just a few days before the wedding. On June 2, 1886, President Cleveland worked as usual. That evening, at 7:00 p.m., the Reverend Byron Sunderland presided over their small wedding ceremony in the Blue Room of the White House (the President's brother, Reverend William Cleveland, assisted). Cleveland was the only President to get married in the White House, and Frances became the youngest First Lady ever. Their first child was Ruth, who was born in 1891, between her father's two terms as President; she died suddenly of diphtheria in 1904. Esther, in 1893, was the only child of a President to be born in the White House. Marion was born in 1895 in Massachusetts. Richard Folsom (1897) and Francis Grover (1903) were born after Grover retired from the Presidency. Following Grover's death in 1908, Frances married Thomas J. Preston—a professor of archeology at Princeton University—in 1913 (she was the first Presidential widow to remarry). Following her death on October 29, 1947, she was buried next to Grover in Princeton.

3. EDITH BOLLING was born on October 15, 1872, in Virginia. In 1896, she married jeweler Norman Galt in Washington, DC. Galt died in 1908. President Woodrow Wilson's first wife, Ellen Louise Axson, died in the White House on August 6, 1914. Following Ellen's death, Wilson's cousin Helen Bones assisted with White House hostessing duties. In March 1915, Bones introduced Wilson to Edith, and he invited her to stay for tea, taking an instant liking to her. He proposed in May, and she accepted in July, but they kept the engagement secret until October. Even with the delay, there was much gossip about the President's quick engagement. Their wedding was a small affair at her home on December 18, 1915; the bride was 43, the groom was 58. She moved easily into the role of First Lady and led by example during World War I, observing rationing days and bringing in a flock of sheep to graze on the White House lawn, to save the manpower of mowing it (and then auctioning the sheep's wool to benefit the Red Cross). Following the President's stroke in September 1919, she screened all business coming before him and kept everyone from seeing the bedridden President. In March 1921, they retired from

the White House to their home on S Street in Washington, where Edith nursed Wilson until his death three years later. Edith remained active in the Washington social scene and directed the Woodrow Wilson Foundation. In 1961, she attended President Kennedy's inauguration. She died of congestive heart failure on December 28, 1961, and was buried next to Wilson in the Washington Cathedral.

38. The Five Longest Presidential Marriages

The longest Presidential marriages naturally skew toward the longest-lived Presidents and First Ladies, but they also combine with those who married younger. Thus, we don't see some of the longest-lived on this list.

1. GEORGE H.W. and BARBARA BUSH. 19-year-old Barbara Pierce married 20-year-old war veteran George H.W. Bush on January 6, 1945. They had six children between 1946 and 1959 (one of whom died as a child). George took office as President days after their 44th anniversary. They retired from Washington four years later, when he was defeated by Bill Clinton, but eight years after that, they became only the second Presidential couple (the first to both live long enough) to see their son—George W. Bush—elected President. The Bushes are only the second couple to live long enough to see their son retire from the Presidency (the first, Joseph and Rose Kennedy, lived through their son's assassination in office). At this writing, the Bushes are days away from celebrating their 71st anniversary.

2. JIMMY and ROSALYNN CARTER. Marrying a month before her 19th birthday, Rosalynn was the third-youngest Presidential wife to marry. Jimmy is three years older. They were married on July 7, 1946, a year and a half after the Bushes. Jimmy took office as President 34-and-a-half years after their wedding. At this writing, the Carters have been married more than 69 years.

3. GERALD and BETTY FORD. The longest-lived President and the third longest-lived First Lady, the Fords married on October 15, 1948, when he was 35 and she was 30 years old (it was her second marriage). Gerald succeeded to the Presidency upon Richard Nixon's resignation, two months before their 26th anniversary. They were married 58 years, 72 days, until Gerald's death in 2006.

4. HARRY and BESS TRUMAN. The fifth longest-lived President and the longest-lived First Lady, the Trumans married on June 28, 1919, when he was 35 and she was 34 years old. Harry succeeded to the Presidency upon Franklin Roosevelt's death, just before their 26th anniversary. They were married 53 years, 181 days, until Harry's death in 1972.

5. RICHARD and PAT NIXON. The Nixons married on June 21, 1940, when he was 27 and she was 28 years old. Richard was elected Vice President during their 13th year of marriage and President 16 years later. Pat died a day after their 53rd anniversary in 1993.

Almosts:

DWIGHT and MAMIE EISENHOWER were married on July 1, 1916 (he was 25; she was 19). They were married 52 years, 270 days, until his death in 1969.

RONALD and NANCY REAGAN were married March 4, 1952 (he was 41 and had been divorced; she was 30). They were married 52 years, 93 days, until his death in 2004 as the (at that time) longest-lived President.

39. The Five Briefest Presidential Marriages

1. THEODORE and ALICE ROOSEVELT. 19-year-old Alice married Theodore on his 22nd birthday, October 27, 1880. On February 12, 1884, Alice gave birth to their daughter, also named Alice, and two days later, she died of Bright's disease and complications from the birth. Their marriage lasted three years, 110 days. Theodore remarried three years later, to Edith, who had been in attendance at his first marriage. Their marriage lasted 32 years.

2. BENJAMIN and MARY HARRISON. The 62-year-old former President married his first wife's 38-year-old niece on April 6, 1896. Caroline, his first wife, died a week before he lost his bid for reelection as President, in 1892. Benjamin and Mary had one child together before his death in 1901 ended their marriage after four years, 341 days.

3. WOODROW and EDITH WILSON. After the death of his first wife the year before, Woodrow Wilson became the third President to marry while in office, when he married 43-year-old widow Edith on December 18, 1915 (10 days before his 59th birthday). They were married eight years, 47 days, until his death in early 1924.

4. RONALD REAGAN and JANE WYMAN. Actor Ronald Reagan married actress Jane Wyman on January 26, 1940, 11 days before his 29th birthday and 21 days after her 23rd. They had two children and adopted a third before they divorced in 1949. Their nine-year marriage is the only one on this list to not end in a death. To date, he is the only divorced man to be elected President. He died in 2004, she in 2007.

5. JOHN and JACQUELINE KENNEDY. On September 12, 1953, 36-year-old Senator John Kennedy married 24-year-old photojournalist Jacqueline.

Seven years later, he was elected President. They had been married 10 years, 71 days, when he was assassinated in November 1963.

Almosts:

THOMAS and MARTHA JEFFERSON. Married on January 1, 1772 (he was 28; she was a 24-year-old widow), she died in 1782, after 10 years, 248 days of marriage.

MARTIN and HANNAH VAN BUREN. Married on February 21, 1807 (he was 24; she would turn 24 in 15 days), she died in 1819, 16 days before their 12th anniversary.

40. The First Ladies Who Died While Their Husbands Were President

1. LETITIA CHRISTIAN TYLER. Her husband, John Tyler (1841–45), was the first Vice President to succeed to the Presidency upon the death of his predecessor (William Henry Harrison). He was also the first President to be widowed while in office. Letitia was born November 12, 1790, married John on March 29, 1813, and bore him eight children by 1830. In 1839, she suffered a paralytic stroke that left her an invalid. While her husband was President, she remained in the upstairs living quarters, coming down to the public areas of the White House only once: for her daughter Elizabeth's wedding in January 1842. She suffered another stroke later that year and died September 10, 1842.

2. CAROLINE LAVINIA SCOTT HARRISON. Her husband, Benjamin Harrison (1889–93), was the first grandson of a President (William Henry Harrison) to be elected President. Caroline was born October 1, 1832, 10 months before her future husband. She married Benjamin on October 20, 1853, and they had two children. She was the first President General of the Daughters of the American Revolution. During her husband's reelection campaign, in 1892, she contracted tuberculosis. She died of it on October 25, 1892, two weeks before election day (he lost).

3. ELLEN LOUISE AXSON WILSON. Her husband, Woodrow Wilson (1913–21), nearly died himself while he was President. Ellen was born May 15, 1860, and married Woodrow on June 24, 1885. She had three daughters and arranged White House weddings for two of them (Jessie married Assistant Secretary of State Francis Sayre in November 1913; Eleanor married Secretary of the Treasury William McAdoo in May 1914). She died of Bright's disease on August 6, 1914.

41. The Presidential Wives Who Missed Their Husbands' Presidencies

Most of the women on this list predeceased their husbands, dying before their husbands became President, but some of them missed their husbands' Presidencies for other reasons.

1. MARTHA WAYLES SKELTON JEFFERSON. Martha was a 23-year-old widow when she married Thomas Jefferson on January 1, 1772. Together, they had six children (although only two lived to adulthood) before she died on September 6, 1782, most probably due to the stresses on her body from the birth of her sixth child (who did not survive) four months earlier. Thomas was elected the third President in the election of 1800 and never remarried.

2. RACHEL DONELSON ROBARDS JACKSON. After divorcing her first husband, 26-year-old Rachel legally married Andrew Jackson on January 17, 1794 (they first thought they had married in 1791, but her divorce was not yet final at that point). In November 1828, Jackson was elected the seventh President, after a campaign in which his marriage to an already-married woman was an issue. The stresses of the campaign resulted in Rachel's death on December 22, 1828, 72 days before Andrew was inaugurated.

3. HANNAH HOES VAN BUREN. Hannah married her childhood sweetheart, Martin Van Buren, on November 21, 1807, two weeks before her 24th birthday. She died of tuberculosis on February 5, 1819, more than 14 years before Martin became Vice President in the election of 1832 and 18 years before he was sworn in as President, after he won the election of 1836. He never remarried.

4. ELLEN "NELL" LEWIS HERNDON ARTHUR. Ellen married Chester Alan Arthur on October 25, 1859, when she was 22 and he was 30. Ellen died of

pneumonia on January 12, 1880. Later that year, Chester was elected Vice President with James Garfield, and when Garfield died two months after being shot, Arthur became President on September 20, 1881. He served out the remainder of the term, retired, and died in November 1886, six years after Ellen.

5. ALICE HATHAWAY LEE ROOSEVELT. Eighteen-year-old Alice married Theodore Roosevelt on his 22nd birthday, and together they had one daughter whom they named Alice. Mrs. Roosevelt died on February 14, 1884, two days after their daughter's birth, devastating Theodore (his mother died the same day, in the same house). Nearly three years later, Theodore married Edith Kermit Carow, a friend who had attended his first wedding. They were together through his Vice Presidency (in 1901), his Presidency (1901–09), his unsuccessful reelection campaign (1912), and his death (January 6, 1919).

6. SARAH JANE FAULKS, later known as Jane Wyman. The 26-year-old actress Jane Wyman married the 28-year-old actor Ronald Reagan on January 26, 1940. They divorced nine years later, and Wyman went on to have a long and successful acting career. Reagan married another actress, Nancy Davis (born Anne Frances Robbins) on March 4, 1952, before he began his political career. He was President of the Screen Actors Guild, then Governor of California in the 1960s, and then elected President in 1980. Wyman outlived Reagan, who died in June 2004.

Two Presidents married after they retired from the Presidency, and the following women were married to men who were retired Presidents.

1. CAROLINE CARMICHAEL MCINTOSH FILLMORE. Millard Fillmore's first wife, Abigail Powers, died a little less than a month after he left office in 1853, having taken ill at Fillmore's successor's inaugural celebrations. Five years later, Millard married Caroline, on February 10, 1858. They were together until Millard's death on March 8, 1874. Caroline died on August 11, 1881.

2. MARY SCOTT LORD DIMMICK HARRISON. Mary, born on April 30, 1858, was the niece of Benjamin Harrison's first wife, Caroline Lavinia Scott Harrison, and she moved into the White House to help with hostessing duties when her aunt became ill. Caroline died days before Benjamin lost the election of 1892. After he retired from office, Mary and Benjamin fell in love, and the 62-year-old former President married his 37-year-old bride on April 6, 1896, much to the consternation of his grown children, who were older than their new stepmother. Mary and Benjamin were together until his death on March 13, 1901. Mary survived him by nearly 47 years, dying on January 5, 1948.

ANNA TUTHILL SYMMES HARRISON was alive during her husband's Presidency, but she wasn't with him for it. William Henry Harrison caught pneumonia during his inaugural speech on March 4, 1841. The weather that year was bad, and Anna had planned to join William in Washington later in the spring, when the weather improved. Instead, she was at their home in Ohio during her husband's one month as President and wasn't able to be with him when he died in the White House on April 4, 1841.

42. The First Ladies Whose Parents Lived to See Them Become First Ladies

NANCY DAVIS REAGAN is the only First Lady to have had two living parents when her husband became President. Her father, Kenneth Robbins, died in 1972, but her mother had divorced him when Nancy was very young. Nancy's mother, Edith Luckett, was born in 1888, and her second husband, Loyal Davis (born in 1896) was Nancy's adoptive father. They both lived to see her become First Lady, and both died while she lived in the White House. Loyal died August 19, 1983, and Edith died October 26, 1987.

Fourteen other First Ladies had one parent live to see their daughters become First Lady:

JULIA GARDINER TYLER (1844–45): her mother, Julia McLachlin Gardiner (1799–1864).

JULIA DENT GRANT (1869–77): her father, Frederick Fayette Dent (October 6, 1786–December 15, 1873).

LUCRETIA RUDOLPH GARFIELD (1881): her father, Zebulon Rudolph (1803–95).

FRANCES FOLSOM CLEVELAND (1886–89, 1893–97): her mother, Emma Cornelia Harmon Folsom (November 12, 1840–December 27, 1915).

CAROLINE SCOTT HARRISON (1889–92): her father, John Witherspoon Scott (January 22, 1800–November 29, 1892), outlived her by one month.

HELEN HERRON TAFT (1909–13): her father, John Williamson Herron (May 10, 1827–August 6, 1912).

EDITH BOLLING GALT WILSON (1915–21): her mother, Sallie White Bolling (January 5, 1843–November 21, 1925).

BESS WALLACE TRUMAN (1945–53): her mother, Margaret Gates Wallace (1855–December 5, 1952).

MAMIE DOUD EISENHOWER (1953–61): her mother, Elivera Mathilda Carlson Doud (May 13, 1878–September 28, 1960).

JACQUELINE BOUVIER KENNEDY (1961–63): her mother, Janet Lee Bouvier (December 3, 1906–July 22, 1989).

ROSALYNN SMITH CARTER (1977–81): her mother, Frances Allethea Murray (December 24, 1905–April 1, 2000)

HILLARY RODHAM CLINTON (1993–2001): her mother, Dorothy Howell Rodham (June 4, 1919–November 1, 2011).

LAURA WELCH BUSH (2001–09): her mother, Jenna Louise Hawkins Welch (born July 24, 1919).

MICHELLE OBAMA (2009–): her mother, Marian Shields Robinson (born July 30, 1937).

43. The First Ladies
Who Were Related to Each Other

This list only discusses the closest relationship, though in many cases, pairs of First Ladies are related through multiple lines of descent.

MARTHA WASHINGTON and ABIGAIL ADAMS were 15th cousins, once removed. Martha's maternal great(14)-grandparents, King Edward I of England (1239–1307) and Eleanor de Castille (1241–90), were Abigail's paternal great(15)-grandparents. Martha was descended through their daughter Joan Plantagenet (also known as Joan of Acre), while Abigail was descended through their daughter Elizabeth Plantagenet.

MARTHA WASHINGTON and LETITIA TYLER were second cousins, twice removed. Martha's maternal great-grandparents, Gideon Macon (1654–1702) and Martha Woodward, were Letitia's paternal great(3)-grandparents. Martha was descended through their daughter Martha Macon (1687–1719), while Letitia was descended through their daughter Amy Macon (born in 1678).

MARTHA WASHINGTON and JULIA GRANT were 13th cousins, five times removed. Martha's maternal great(12)-grandmother was Eleanor De Clare (1292–1337), who was Julia's paternal great(17)-grandmother. Martha was descended through her daughter Elizabeth Le De Spencer via her first husband, Hugh Le De Spencer (died in 1326), while Julia was descended through her daughter Joyce La Zouche (1327–72) via her second husband, William La Zouche (died in 1336).

MARTHA WASHINGTON and LUCRETIA GARFIELD were 13th cousins, five times removed. Martha's maternal great(12)-grandparents, Eleanor De Clare (1292–1337) and Hugh Le De Spencer (died in 1326), were Lucretia's great(17)-grandparents. Martha was descended through their daughter Elizabeth Le De Spencer, while Lucretia was descended through their daughter Isabel Le De Spencer.

MARTHA WASHINGTON and ELLEN ARTHUR were 13th cousins, four times removed. Martha's maternal great(12)-grandparents, Eleanor De Clare (1292–1337) and Hugh Le De Spencer (died in 1326), were Ellen's great(16)-grandparents. Martha was descended through their daughter Elizabeth Le De Spencer, while Ellen was descended through their son Edward Le De Spencer.

MARTHA WASHINGTON and ELLEN WILSON were 13th cousins, six times removed. Martha's maternal great(12)-grandparents, Hugh Le De Spencer and Eleanor De Clare, were Ellen's paternal great(18)-grandparents. Martha was descended through their daughter Elizabeth Le De Spencer, while Ellen was descended through their daughter Isabel Le De Spencer.

MARTHA WASHINGTON and EDITH WILSON were first cousins, five times removed. Martha's paternal grandparents, John Dandridge (1655–1731) and Ann Matthews, were Edith's paternal great(5)-grandparents. Martha was descended through their son John Dandridge (1700–56), who was her father, while Edith was descended through their son William Dandridge (died in 1743).

MARTHA WASHINGTON and MAMIE EISENHOWER were half-15th cousins, 10 times removed, or 16th cousins, 10 times removed. Martha's maternal great(14)-grandfather, King Edward I of England (1239–1307), was Mamie's paternal great(24)-grandfather. Martha was descended through his daughter Joan Plantagent (aka Joan of Acre) with Eleanor de Castille (1241–90), while Mamie was descended through his son Thomas Plantagenet (1300–38) with Marguerite of France.

ABIGAIL ADAMS and MARTHA JEFFERSON were 15th cousins. Abigail's maternal great(14)-grandparents, Bartholomew Bartlesmere and Margaret

De Clare, were Martha's maternal great(14)-grandparents. Abigail was descended through their daughter Elizabeth Badlesmere, while Martha was descended through their daughter Margaret Badlesmere.

ABIGAIL ADAMS and ANNA HARRISON were half-20th cousins, or 21st cousins. Abigail's great(19)-grandfather, Richard De Clare (1130–76), was Anna's paternal great(19)-grandfather. Abigail was descended through his daughter Isabel De Clare (1171–1220) by his wife Eva MacMurrough (died in 1177), while Anna was descended through his son Roger "The Good" De Clare by his wife Alice De Meschines.

ABIGAIL ADAMS and JANE PIERCE were half-14th cousins, twice removed, or 15th cousins, twice removed. Abigail's maternal great(15)-grandmother, Isabel de Beauchamp (1249–1306), was Jane's paternal great(13)-grandmother. Abigail was descended through her daughter Maud De Chaworth (born in 1282) via her second husband, Patrick De Chaworth (born in 1250), while Jane was descended through her son Sir Walter Le Blount (1277–1315) via her first husband, Sir William Le Blount (1233–80).

ABIGAIL ADAMS and MARY LINCOLN were 13th cousins, three times removed. Abigail's maternal great(12)-grandparents, John of Gaunt Beaufort (1340–98/9) and Catherine (or Katherine) Roet (1350–1403), were Mary's maternal great(15)-grandparents. Abigail was descended through their son Henry Beaufort (1367–1447), while Mary was descended through their son Sir John Beaufort (1371–1410).

ABIGAIL ADAMS and JULIA GRANT were half-16th cousins, four times removed, or 17th cousins, four times removed. Abigail's paternal great(15)-grandfather, King Edward I of England (1239–1307), was Julia's paternal great(19)-grandfather. Abigail was descended through his daughter Elizabeth Plantagenet by his first wife, Eleanor de Castille (1241-90), while Julia was descended through his son John De Botetorte (1265–1324) and his mistress Alice Lusignan.

ABIGAIL ADAMS and LUCRETIA GARFIELD were 16th cousins, four times removed. Abigail's paternal great(15)-grandparents, King Edward I of England (1239–1307) and Eleanor de Castille (1241–90), were Lucretia's great(19)-grandparents. Abigail was descended through their daughter Elizabeth Plantagenet, while Lucretia was descended through their daughter Joan Plantagenet (also known as Joan of Acre).

ABIGAIL ADAMS and ELLEN ARTHUR were 13th cousins, once removed. Abigail's maternal great(12)-grandparents, John of Gaunt Beaufort (1340–98/9) and Catherine (or Katherine) Roet (1350–1403), were Ellen's great(13)-grandparents. Abigail was descended through their son Henry Beaufort (1367–1447), while Ellen was descended through their daughter Joan Beaufort (also known as Joan of Lancaster).

ABIGAIL ADAMS and HELEN TAFT were 23rd cousins, three times removed. Abigail's maternal great(25)-grandparents, Alfgar III, Earl of Mercia, and his wife Elfgifu, were Helen's maternal great(22)-grandparents. Abigail was descended through their daughter Edith, Duchess of Mercia, while Helen was descended through their daughter Lucy of Mercia (born in 1040).

ABIGAIL ADAMS and ELLEN WILSON were 16th cousins, five times removed. Abigail's paternal great(15)-grandparents, King Edward I of England (1239–1307) and Eleanor de Castille (1241–90), were Ellen's paternal great(20)-grandparents. Abigail was descended through their daughter Elizabeth Plantagenet, while Ellen was descended through their daughter Joan Plantagenet (also known as Joan of Acre).

ABIGAIL ADAMS and EDITH WILSON were 13th cousins, three times removed. Abigail's maternal great(12)-grandparents, John of Gaunt Beaufort (1340–98/9) and Catherine (or Katherine) Roet (1350–1403), were Edith's paternal great(15)-grandparents. Abigail was descended through their son Henry Beaufort (1367–1447), while Edith was descended through both their daughter Joan Beaufort and their son Sir John Beaufort (1371–1410).

ABIGAIL ADAMS and ELEANOR ROOSEVELT were 13th cousins, three times removed. Abigail's maternal great(12)-grandparents, John of Gaunt Beaufort (1340–98/9) and Catherine (or Katherine) Roet (1350–1403), were Eleanor's paternal great(15)-grandparents. Abigail was descended through their son Henry Beaufort (1367–1447), while Eleanor was descended from their son Sir John Beaufort (1371–1410).

ABIGAIL ADAMS and MAMIE EISENHOWER were 11th cousins, eight times removed. Abigail's maternal great(10)-grandparents, Sir Thomas Stanley (c1406–59) and Joan Goushill, were Mamie's paternal great(18)-grandparents. Abigail was descended through their daughter Lady Margaret Stanley, while Mamie was descended through their daughter Catherine Stanley.

ABIGAIL ADAMS and BARBARA BUSH are 13th cousins, four times removed. Abigail's maternal great(12)-grandparents, Sir John Fitz Alan and Eleanor Maltovers (1345–1405), are Barbara's paternal great(16)-grandparents. Abigail was descended through their daughter Eleanor Fitz Alan, while Barbara is descended through their daughter Joan Fitz Alan.

ABIGAIL ADAMS and LAURA BUSH are 19th cousins, eight times removed. Abigail's great(18)-grandparents, King Henry II (1133–89) and Eleanor De Aquitaine (1122–1204), are Laura's paternal great(26)-grandparents. Abigail was descended through their son King John (1166–1216), while Laura is descended through their daughter Joan.

MARTHA JEFFERSON and LUCRETIA GARFIELD were 16th cousins, five times removed. Martha's maternal great(15)-grandparents, Roger De Quincy (1174–1264) and Helen of Galloway (also known as Helen McDonald), were Lucretia's maternal great(20)-grandparents. Martha was descended through their daughter Helen De Quincy, while Lucretia was descended through their daughter Elizabeth De Quincy.

MARTHA JEFFERSON and NANCY REAGAN are 14th cousins, seven times removed. Martha's maternal great(13)-grandparents, Eudes La Zouche and Millicent De Cantelupe, are Nancy's paternal great(20)-grandparents. Martha was descended through their daughter Lucy La Zouche, while Nancy is descended through their daughter Elizabeth La Zouche.

MARTHA JEFFERSON and BARBARA BUSH are 14th cousins, seven times removed. Martha's maternal great(13)-grandparents, Eudes La Zouche and Millicent De Cantelupe, are Barbara's paternal great(20)-grandparents. Martha was descended through their daughter Lucy La Zouche, while Barbara is descended through their daughter Eva La Zouche.

DOLLEY MADISON and MARY LINCOLN were 11th cousins, five times removed. Dolley's paternal great(10)-grandparents, King James I of Scotland and Joan Beaufort, were Mary's maternal great(15)-grandparents. Dolley was descended through their son King James II, while Mary was descended through their daughter Joan, Princess of Scotland.

DOLLEY MADISON and ELLEN ARTHUR were third cousins, twice removed. Dolley's maternal great-great-grandparents, Cornelius Dabney and Sarah Jennings, were Ellen's paternal great(4)-grandparents. Dolley was descended through their daughter Sarah Dabney, while Ellen was descended through their daughter Mary Dabney.

DOLLEY MADISON and EDITH WILSON were second cousins, three times removed. Dolley's paternal great-grandparents, George Payne (1679–1744) and Mary Woodson (1678–1766), were Edith's paternal great(4)-grandparents. Dolley was descended through their son Josiah Payne (1705–84), while Edith was descended through their son John Payne (1713–84).

DOLLEY MADISON and ELEANOR ROOSEVELT were 10th cousins, four times removed. Dolley's great(9)-grandparents, Robert Fleming and Lady Janet Douglas, were Eleanor's paternal great(13)-grandparents. Dolley was descended through their son Malcolm Fleming, while Eleanor was descended through their daughter Beatrice Elizabeth Fleming.

ELIZABETH MONROE and FRANCES CLEVELAND were third cousins, five times removed. Elizabeth's maternal great-great-grandparents, James Sands (1622–95) and Sarah Walker (1626–1709), were Frances's maternal great(7)-grandparents. Elizabeth was descended through their son James Sands, while Frances was descended through their daughter Mercy Sands.

ELIZABETH MONROE and GRACE COOLIDGE were fourth cousins, three times removed. Elizabeth's maternal great(3)-grandparents, Stephen Deane (1606–34) and Elizabeth Ring (1602–87), were Grace's maternal great(6)-grandparents. Elizabeth was descended through their son Christopher Deane (1632–89), while Grace was descended through their daughter Miriam Deane (1633–1706).

HANNAH VAN BUREN and ELEANOR ROOSEVELT were fourth cousins, three times removed. Hannah's paternal great(3)-grandparents, Luykas Gerritsen Wyndgard and Anna Van Hoesen, were Eleanor's paternal great(6)-grandparents. Hannah was descended through their daughter Elizabeth Lucasse Wyndgard, while Eleanor was descended through their daughter Margaret Lucasse Wyndgard.

ANNA HARRISON and JULIA TYLER were fifth cousins, once removed. Anna's maternal great(4)-grandparents, William King (1595–1650) and Dorothy Hayne (born in 1601), were Julia's paternal great(5)-grandparents. Anna was descended through their daughter Deliverance King (1641–89), while Julia was descended through their son Samuel King.

ANNA HARRISON and ELLEN ARTHUR were 21st cousins, three times removed. Anna's paternal great(20)-grandparents, Ranulf III De Meschines (1070–1129) and Lucy Taillebois (1072–1136), were Ellen's paternal great(23)-grandparents. Anna was descended through their daughter Alice de Meschines, while Ellen was descended through their son Ranulf IV De Meschines.

ANNA HARRISON and ALICE ROOSEVELT were fourth cousins, five times removed. Anna's paternal great(3)-grandparents, Zachariah Symmes (1599–1671) and Sarah Baker (1605–73), were Alice's paternal great(8)-grandparents. Anna was descended through their son William Symmes (1626/28–1705), while Alice was descended through their daughter Mary Symmes.

ANNA HARRISON and EDITH ROOSEVELT were fifth cousins, three times removed. Anna's maternal great(4)-grandparents, Joseph Horton (1578–1640) and Mary Schuyler, were Edith's maternal great(7)-grandparents. Anna was descended through their son Barnabas Horton (1600–84), while Edith was descended through their son Thomas Horton (1596–1640).

ANNA HARRISON and HELEN TAFT were 21st cousins, five times removed. Anna's paternal great(20)-grandparents, Ranulf III De Meschines (1070–1129) and Lucy Taillebois (1072–1136), were Helen's maternal great(25)-grandparents. Anna was descended through their daughter Alice de Meschines, while Helen was descended through their son Ranulf IV De Meschines.

ANNA HARRISON and BESS TRUMAN were 10th cousins, six times removed. Anna's paternal great(9)-grandparents, John Fortescue (1420–80) and Jane Preston, were Bess's maternal great(15)-grandparents. Anna was descended through their daughter Joan Fortescue, while Bess was descended through their son William Fortescue.

ANNA HARRISON and JANE WYMAN (Reagan) were second cousins, five times removed. Anna's maternal great-grandparents, Caleb Horton (1687–1722) and Phebe Terry (1690–1776), were Jane's maternal great(6)-grandparents. Anna was descended through their daughter Phoebe Horton (1722–1793), while Jane was descended through their son Nathaniel Horton (1719–1804).

ANNA HARRISON and BARBARA BUSH are 21st cousins, five times removed. Anna's paternal great(20)-grandparents, Ranulf III De Meschines (1070–1129) and

Lucy Taillebois (1072–1136), are Barbara's paternal great(25)-grandparents. Anna was descended through their daughter Alice de Meschines, while Barbara is descended through their son Ranulf IV De Meschines.

MARGARET TAYLOR and JULIA GRANT were third cousins, twice removed. Margaret's paternal great-great-grandparents, Walter Smith (1667–1711) and Rachel Hall (1671–1730), were Julia's paternal great(4)-grandparents. Margaret was descended through their son Walter Smith, while Julia was descended through their daughter Lucy Smith (1686–1770).

JANE PIERCE and LUCRETIA GARFIELD were 11th cousins, twice removed. Jane's paternal great(10)-grandparents, Sir Walter Le Blount (1350–1403) and Sacha De Ayala (1360–1418), were Lucretia's maternal great(12)-grandparents. Jane was descended through their daughter Constance Blount (born in 1385), while Lucretia was descended through their son Thomas Blount (1373–1456).

JANE PIERCE and ELLEN ARTHUR were 13th cousins, twice removed. Jane's paternal great(12)-grandparents, John Bedelgate and Mary De Beauchamp, were Ellen's paternal great(14)-grandparents. Jane was descended through their daughter Elizabeth Bedelgate (born in 1390), while Ellen was descended through their daughter Joan Bedelgate.

JANE PIERCE and BARBARA BUSH are 12th cousins, eight times removed. Jane's paternal great(11)-grandparents, Maurice De Berkeley (1271–1326) and Eva La Zouche, are Barbara's paternal great(19)-grandparents. Jane was descended through their son Thomas De Berkeley (1298–1368), while Barbara is descended through their daughter Millicent De Berkeley.

MARY LINCOLN and LUCY HAYES were fifth cousins, once removed. Mary's paternal great(4)-grandparents, Nathaniel Merriman (1613–94) and Joan Lines (1628–1709), were Lucy's paternal great(5)-grandparents. Mary was descended through their son John Merriman (1660–1741), while Lucy was descended through their son Caleb Merriman (1665–1703).

MARY LINCOLN and ELLEN ARTHUR were 14th cousins, twice removed. Mary's maternal great(15)-grandparents, John of Gaunt Beaufort (1340–98/9) and Katherine (or Catherine) Roet (1350–1403), were Ellen's paternal great(13)-grandparents. Mary was descended through their son John De Beaufort, while Ellen was descended through their daughter Joan Beaufort.

MARY LINCOLN and ALICE ROOSEVELT were eighth cousins, twice removed. Mary's maternal great(7)-grandparents, Edward Bulkeley and Olive Irby, were Alice's paternal great(9)-grandparents. Mary was descended through their son Rev. Peter Bulkeley, while Alice was descended through their daughter Martha Bulkeley (1572–1639).

MARY LINCOLN and EDITH WILSON were eighth cousins, once removed. Mary's paternal great(7)-grandparents, William Maule (1545–1619) and Bethia Guthrie, were Edith's paternal great(8)-grandparents. Mary was descended through their daughter Isabel Maule, while Edith was descended through their daughter Eleanor Maule.

MARY LINCOLN and ELEANOR ROOSEVELT were 10th cousins, four times removed. Mary's paternal great(9)-grandparents, Colin Campbell and Isabel Stewart, were Eleanor's paternal great(13)-grandparents. Mary was descended through their daughter Helen Campbell, while Eleanor was descended through their son Archibald Campbell.

MARY LINCOLN and MAMIE EISENHOWER were 15th cousins, three times removed. Mary's maternal great(14)-grandparents, Sir John Beaufort (1371–1410) and Margaret De Holland, were Mamie's paternal great(17)-grandparents. Mary was descended through their daughter Joan De Beaufort, while Mamie was descended through their son Edmund Beaufort.

MARY LINCOLN and BARBARA BUSH are fifth cousins, three times removed. Mary Lincoln's maternal great(4)-grandparents, John Peck (1640–91) and Mary Moss (1644–1725), are Barbara's paternal great(7)-grandparents.

Mary was descended through their daughter Elizabeth Peck (1673–1709), while Barbara is descended through their son John Peck (1671–1768).

JULIA GRANT and LUCRETIA GARFIELD were half-18th cousins, or 19th cousins. Julia's paternal great(17)-grandmother, Eleanor De Clare (1292–1337), was Lucretia's great(17)-grandmother. Julia was descended through her daughter Joyce La Zouche (1327–72) via her second husband, William La Zouche (died in 1336), while Lucretia was descended through her daughter Isabel Le De Spencer via her first husband, Hugh Le De Spencer (died in 1326).

JULIA GRANT and ELLEN ARTHUR were half-17th cousins, once removed, or 18th cousins, once removed. Julia's paternal great(17)-grandmother, Eleanor De Clare (1292–1337), was Ellen's great(16)-grandmother. Julia was descended through her daughter Joyce La Zouche (1327–72) via her second husband, William La Zouche (died in 1336), while Ellen was descended through her son Edward Le De Spencer with her first husband, Hugh Le De Spencer (died in 1326).

JULIA GRANT and ELLEN WILSON were half-20th cousins, once removed, or 21st cousins, once removed. Julia's paternal great(19)-grandfather, King Edward I of England (1239–1307), was Ellen's paternal great(20)-grandfather. Julia was descended through his illegitimate son John De Botetorte (1265–1324) with Alice Lusignan, while Lucretia was descended through his daughter Joan Plantagenet (also known as Joan of Acre) with Eleanor de Castille (1241–90).

JULIA GRANT and MAMIE EISENHOWER were half-20th cousins, five times removed, or 21st cousins, five times removed. Julia's paternal great(19)-grandfather, King Edward I of England (1239–1307), was Mamie's paternal great(24)-grandfather. Julia was descended through his illegitimate son John De Botetorte (1265–1324) with Alice Lusignan, while Mamie was descended through his son Thomas Plantagenet (1300–38) with Marguerite of France.

LUCRETIA GARFIELD and ELLEN ARTHUR were 17th cousins, once removed. Lucretia's great(17)-grandparents, Hugh Le De Spencer (died in 1326) and Eleanor De Clare (1292–1337), were Ellen's great(16)-grandparents. Lucretia was descended through their daughter Isabel Le De Spencer, while Ellen was descended through their son Edward Le De Spencer.

LUCRETIA GARFIELD and ELLEN WILSON were 18th cousins, once removed. Lucretia's great(17)-grandparents, Hugh Le De Spencer and Eleanor (or Alainore) De Clare, were Ellen's paternal great(18)-grandparents. Lucretia was descended through their son Hugh Le De Spencer (1260–1326), while Ellen was descended through their daughter Isabel Le De Spencer.

LUCRETIA GARFIELD and MAMIE EISENHOWER were half-20th cousins, five times removed, or 21st cousins, five times removed. Lucretia's great(19)-grandfather, King Edward I of England (1239–1307), was Mamie's paternal great(24)-grandfather. Lucretia was descended through his daughter Joan Plantagent (also known as Joan of Acre) with Eleanor de Castille (1241–90), while Mamie was descended through his son Thomas Plantagenet (1300–38) with Marguerite of France.

LUCRETIA GARFIELD and BARBARA BUSH are 21st cousins, twice removed. Lucretia's maternal great(20)-grandparents, Roger De Quincy (1174–1264) and Helen of Galloway (also known as Helen McDonald), are Barbara's paternal great(22)-grandparents. Lucretia was descended through their daughter Elizabeth De Quincy, while Barbara is descended through their daughter Helen De Quincy.

ELLEN ARTHUR and HELEN TAFT were 22nd cousins, twice removed. Ellen's paternal great(21)-grandparents, Hugh De Meschines and Bertrade De Montfort, were Helen's maternal great(23)-grandparents. Ellen was descended through their daughter Hawise De Meschines, while Helen was descended through their daughter Mabel De Meschines (born in 1123).

ELLEN ARTHUR and EDITH WILSON were half-12th cousins, twice removed, or 13th cousins, twice removed. Ellen's paternal great(11)-grandfather, Edward De Neville (1407–76), was Edith's paternal great(13)-grandfather. Ellen was descended from his son George De Neville via his wife Elizabeth De Beauchamp (1415–48), while Edith was descended from his daughter Catherine De Neville via his wife Catherine Howard.

ELLEN ARTHUR and ELEANOR ROOSEVELT were 14th cousins, twice removed. Ellen's paternal great(13)-grandparents, John of Gaunt Beaufort (1340–98/9) and Katherine Roet (1350–1403), were Eleanor's paternal great(15)-grandparents. Ellen was descended through their daughter Joan Beaufort (also known as Joan of Lancaster), while Eleanor was descended through their son John Beaufort.

ELLEN ARTHUR and MAMIE EISENHOWER were 14th cousins, three times removed. Ellen's paternal great(13)-grandparents, Henry Percy and Eleanor De Neville, were Mamie's paternal great(16)-grandparents. Ellen was descended through their son Henry Percy, while Mamie was descended through their daughter Katherine Percy.

ELLEN ARTHUR and BARBARA BUSH are 21st cousins, once removed. Ellen's great(20)-grandparents, William Marshall (1170–1219) and Isabel De Clare (1171–1220), are Barbara's paternal great(21)-grandparents. Ellen was descended through their daughter Isabelle Marshall, while Barbara is descended through their daughter Maud Marshall.

FRANCES CLEVELAND and EDITH ROOSEVELT were seventh cousins, twice removed. Frances's maternal great(8)-grandparents, Robert Blott (died in 1665) and Susanna Selbee, were Edith's maternal great(6)-grandparents. Frances was descended through their daughter Mary, while Edith was descended through their daughter Joanna.

FRANCES CLEVELAND and GRACE COOLIDGE were eighth cousins. Frances's paternal great(7)-grandparents, John Perkins (1583–1654) and Judith

Gater (born in 1588), were Grace's paternal great(7)-grandparents. Frances was descended through their son Abraham Perkins (1613–81), while Grace was descended through their son Thomas Perkins (1622–86).

FRANCES CLEVELAND and BESS TRUMAN were seventh cousins, once removed. Frances's maternal great(6)-grandparents, Isaac Sheldon (1630–1708) and Mary Woodford, were Bess's maternal great(7)-grandparents. Frances was descended through their daughter Mary Sheldon (1654–1728), while Bess was descended through their daughter Mindwell Sheldon.

FRANCES CLEVELAND and NANCY REAGAN are seventh cousins, twice removed. Frances's maternal great(6)-grandparents, Isaac Sheldon and Mary Woodford, are Nancy's paternal great(8)-grandparents. Frances was descended through their daughter Mary, while Nancy is descended through their daughter Ruth.

CAROLINE HARRISON and MARY HARRISON were aunt and niece. Mary's mother, Elizabeth Mayhew Scott, was Caroline's sister.

EDITH ROOSEVELT and BESS TRUMAN were seventh cousins, three times removed. Edith's maternal great(6)-grandparents, Robert Blott (died in 1665) and Susanna Selbee, were Bess's maternal great(9)-grandparents. Edith was descended through their daughter Joanna, while Bess was descended through their son Thomas (died in 1666/7).

HELEN TAFT and BARBARA BUSH are 23rd cousins. Helen's maternal great(22)-grandparents, William De Albini and Mabel De Meschines (born in 1123), were Barbara's paternal great(22)-grandparents. Helen was descended through their daughter Nicole De Albini, while Barbara is descended through their daughter Isabel De Albini.

ELLEN WILSON and BESS TRUMAN were seventh cousins, three times removed. Ellen's maternal great(6)-grandparents, Matthew Allyn (1604–71) and Margaret Wyatt, were Bess's maternal great(9)-grandparents. Ellen was descended through their son Thomas Allyn, while Bess was descended through their daughter Mary Allyn.

ELLEN WILSON and MAMIE EISENHOWER were half-21st cousins, four times removed, or 22nd cousins, four times removed. Ellen's paternal great(20)-grandfather, King Edward I of England (1239–1307), was Mamie's paternal great(24)-grandfather. Ellen was descended through his daughter Joan Plantagent (also known as Joan of Acre) with Eleanor de Castille (1241–90), while Mamie was descended through his son Thomas Plantagenet (1300–38) with Marguerite of France.

ELLEN WILSON and NANCY REAGAN are seventh cousins, three times removed. Ellen's maternal great(6)-grandparents, Matthew Allyn (1604–71) and Margaret Wyatt, are Nancy's paternal great(9)-grandparents. Ellen was descended through their son Thomas Allyn, while Nancy is descended through their daughter Mary Allyn.

EDITH WILSON and ELEANOR ROOSEVELT were 15th cousins. Edith's paternal great(14)-grandparents, Sir John Beaufort (1371–1410) and Margaret De Holland, were Eleanor's paternal great(14)-grandparents. Edith was descended through their son Edmund Beaufort, while Eleanor was descended through their daughter Joan Beaufort.

EDITH WILSON and MAMIE EISENHOWER were 14th cousins, three times removed. Edith's paternal great(13)-grandparents, Edmund Beaufort and Eleanor De Beauchamp, were Mamie's paternal great(16)-grandparents. Edith was descended through their daughter Eleanor Beaufort, while Mamie was descended through their daughter Margaret Beaufort.

FLORENCE HARDING and BARBARA BUSH are eighth cousins, twice removed. Florence's maternal great(7)-grandparents, Edward Marvin (1545–1615) and his wife Margaret, were Barbara's paternal great(9)-grandparents. Florence was descended through their son Matthew Marvin

(1600–78), while Barbara is descended through their son Reinhold Marvin (1593–1662).

GRACE COOLIDGE and LOU HOOVER were seventh cousins, once removed. Grace's paternal great(6)-grandparents, William Cogswell (1619–1700) and Susanna Hawkes (1633–76), were Lou's maternal great(7)-grandparents. Grace was descended through their son John Cogswell (1665–1710), while Lou was descended through their daughter Hester Cogswell.

GRACE COOLIDGE and BARBARA BUSH are seventh cousins, twice removed. Grace's maternal great(6)-grandparents, Thomas Thayer (1596–1665) and Margery Wheeler (1597–1642), are Barbara's paternal great(8)-grandparents. Grace was descended through their son Shadrack Thayer (1629–78), while Barbara is descended through their son Fernando Thayer (1625–1713).

ELEANOR ROOSEVELT and MAMIE EISENHOWER were 15th cousins, three times removed. Eleanor's paternal great(14)-grandparents, Sir John Beaufort (1371–1410) and Margaret De Holland, were Mamie's paternal great(17)-grandparents. Eleanor was descended through their daughter Joan Beaufort, while Mamie was descended through their son Edmund Beaufort.

BESS TRUMAN and NANCY REAGAN are eighth cousins. Bess's maternal great(7)-grandparents, John Moseley (1638–90) and Mary Newberry (1648–1703), are Nancy's paternal great(7)-grandparents. Bess was descended through their son John Moseley, while Nancy is descended through their daughter Mary Moseley (1673–1746).

MAMIE EISENHOWER and JANE WYMAN (Reagan) were 12th cousins, once removed. Mamie's paternal great(12)-grandparents, Richard Baldwin (1503–52) and Ellen Apuke (1507–65), were Jane's maternal great(11)-grandparents. Mamie was descended through their son Henry Baldwin, while Jane was descended through their son Richard Baldwin (1540–1631).

NANCY REAGAN and BARBARA BUSH are 21st cousins. Nancy's paternal great(20)-grandparents, Eudes La Zouche and Millicent De Cantelupe, are Barbara's paternal great(20)-grandparents. Nancy is descended through their daughter Elizabeth La Zouche, while Barbara is descended through their daughter Eva La Zouche.

HANNAH VAN BUREN is only related to one other First Lady, ELEANOR ROOSEVELT.

LETITIA TYLER is only related to MARTHA WASHINGTON.

JULIA TYLER is only related to ANNA HARRISON.

MARGARET TAYLOR is only related to JULIA GRANT.

LUCY HAYES is only related to MARY LINCOLN.

CAROLINE HARRISON and MARY HARRISON are only related to each other (aunt and niece).

EDITH ROOSEVELT is only related to ANNA HARRISON.

FLORENCE HARDING is only related to BARBARA BUSH.

LOU HOOVER is only related to GRACE COOLIDGE.

LAURA BUSH is only related to ABIGAIL ADAMS.

The following First Ladies are, to the best of our knowledge, completely unrelated to any other First Lady: LOUISA ADAMS, RACHEL JACKSON, SARAH POLK, ABIGAIL FILLMORE, CAROLINE FILLMORE, ELIZA JOHNSON, IDA MCKINLEY, JACQUELINE KENNEDY, LADY BIRD JOHNSON, PAT NIXON, BETTY FORD, ROSALYNN CARTER, HILLARY CLINTON, and MICHELLE OBAMA.

44. The First Ladies Who Were Related to Presidents (Other Than Their Husbands)

Many Presidential wives are related to Presidents by blood, including two who were mothers of Presidents and one who was the grandmother of a President. No Presidential daughters, however, have moved back into the White House on their own. The closest was Eleanor Roosevelt, who was President Theodore Roosevelt's niece and married Franklin Roosevelt.

MARTHA WASHINGTON and JOHN QUINCY ADAMS were 15th cousins, twice removed. Martha's maternal great(14)-grandparents, King Edward I of England (1239–1307) and Eleanor de Castille (1241–90), were John's maternal great(16)-grandparents. Martha was descended through their daughter Joan Plantagenet (also known as Joan of Acre), while John was descended through their daughter Elizabeth Plantagenet.

MARTHA WASHINGTON and BARACK OBAMA are 15th cousins, nine times removed. Martha's maternal great(14)-grandparents, King Edward I of England (1239–1307) and Eleanor de Castille (1241–90), are Barack's maternal great(23)-grandparents. Martha was descended through their daughter Joan Plantagenet (also known as Joan of Acre), while Barack is descended through their daughter Elizabeth Plantagenet.

ABIGAIL ADAMS and her husband, JOHN ADAMS, were third cousins. Abigail's paternal great-great-grandparents, Thomas Boylston (c1615–c1653) and Sarah (c1618–1704), were John's maternal great-great-grandparents. Abigail was descended through their daughter Sarah Boylston (1642–1711), while John was descended through their son Thomas Boylston (1645–96).

ABIGAIL ADAMS was JOHN QUINCY ADAMS'S mother.

ABIGAIL ADAMS and BENJAMIN HARRISON were half-20th cousins, twice removed, or 21st cousins, twice removed. Abigail's great(19)-grandfather, Richard De Clare (1130–76), was Benjamin's paternal great(21)-grandfather. Abigail was descended through his daughter Isabel De Clare (1171–1220) by his wife Eva MacMurrough (died in 1177), while Benjamin was descended through his son Roger "The Good" De Clare by his wife Alice De Meschines.

ABIGAIL ADAMS and THEODORE ROOSEVELT were 13th cousins, twice removed. Abigail's maternal great(12)-grandparents, John of Gaunt Beaufort (1340–98/9) and Catherine (or Katherine) Roet (1350–1403), were Theodore's maternal great(14)-grandparents. Abigail was descended through their son Henry Beaufort (1367–1447), while Theodore was descended from their son Sir John Beaufort (1371–1410).

ABIGAIL ADAMS and GEORGE W. BUSH are 13th cousins, five times removed. Abigail's maternal great(12)-grandparents, Sir John Fitz Alan and Eleanor Maltovers (1345–1405), were George's maternal great(17)-grandparents. Abigail was descended through their daughter Eleanor Fitz Alan, while George is descended through their daughter Joan Fitz Alan.

ABIGAIL ADAMS and BARACK OBAMA are 11th cousins, eight times removed. Abigail's maternal great(10)-grandparents, Thomas Stanley (c1406–59) and Joan Goushill, are Barack's maternal great(18)-grandparents. Abigail was descended through their daughter Margaret, while Barack is descended through their daughter Catherine.

MARTHA JEFFERSON and her husband, THOMAS JEFFERSON, were third cousins. Martha's maternal great-great-grandparents, Henry Isham (1628–1675/85) and Katherine Banks (1632–86), were Thomas's maternal great-great-grandparents. Martha was descended through their daughter Anne Isham, while Thomas was descended through their daughter Mary Isham (1658–1735).

MARTHA JEFFERSON and JOHN QUINCY ADAMS were 15th cousins, once removed. Martha's maternal great(14)-grandparents, Bartholomew Bartlesmere and Margaret De Clare, were John's maternal great(15)-grandparents. Martha was descended through their daughter Margaret Badlesmere, while John was descended through their daughter Elizabeth Badlesmere.

MARTHA JEFFERSON and GEORGE W. BUSH are 14th cousins, eight times removed. Martha's maternal great(13)-grandparents, Eudes La Zouche and Millicent De Cantelupe, were George's maternal great(21)-grandparents. Martha was descended through their daughter Lucy La Zouche, while George is descended through their daughter Eva La Zouche.

MARTHA JEFFERSON and BARACK OBAMA are 18th cousins, seven times removed. Martha's maternal great(17)-grandparents, Sir William de Ros and Lucy FitzPiers, are Barack's maternal great(24)-grandparents. Martha is descended through their son Sir Robert de Ros, while Barack is descended through their son Sir William de Ros.

DOLLEY MADISON and JAMES BUCHANAN were half-12th cousins, twice removed, or 13th cousins, twice removed. Dolley's great(11)-grandfather, Robert Stewart, Duke of Albany (1340–1420), was James's paternal great(13)-grandfather. Dolley was descended from his daughter Elizabeth Stewart via his second wife, Muriella de Keith. James was descended from his son Murdoch Stewart, Duke of Albany (1362–1425), via his first wife, Mary Graham.

DOLLEY MADISON and THEODORE ROOSEVELT were 11th cousins, three times removed. Dolley's paternal great(10)-grandparents, Sir James Douglas and Beatrix Sinclair, were Theodore's maternal great(13)-grandparents. Dolley was descended through their daughter Janet Douglas, while Theodore was descended through their son James Douglas.

ELIZABETH MONROE and MARTIN VAN BUREN were third cousins, once removed. Elizabeth's paternal great(3)-grandparents, Matthew Van Deusen and Helena Robberts, were Martin's paternal great-great-grandparents. Elizabeth was descended through their daughter Lysbeth Van Deusen, while Martin was descended through their daughter Marritje Teuwisse Van Deusen.

ELIZABETH MONROE and FRANKLIN ROOSEVELT were half-first cousins, twice removed. Elizabeth's maternal grandfather, John Aspinwall (born in 1704), married Mary (or Sarah) Sands (1708–65) in 1728. Their daughter, Hannah, was Elizabeth's mother. John Aspinwall then married Rebecca Smith (c1735–1809), and their son, John Aspinwall (1774–1847), was Franklin's great-grandfather.

HANNAH VAN BUREN and her husband, MARTIN VAN BUREN, were first cousins, once removed. Hannah's paternal great-grandparents, Johannes Dircksen Hoes (born in 1700) and Jannetje Laurense Van Schaick (born in 1707), were Martin's maternal grandparents. Hannah was descended through their son Dirck Hoes (1724–73), while their daughter Maria Hoes (1748–1817) was Martin's mother.

HANNAH VAN BUREN and THEODORE ROOSEVELT were fourth cousins, twice removed. Hannah's paternal great(3)-grandparents, Luykas Gerritsen Wyndgard and Anna Van Hoesen, were Theodore's paternal great(5)-grandparents. Hannah was descended through their daughter Elizabeth Lucasse Wyndgard, while Theodore was descended through their daughter Margaret Lucasse Wyndgard.

ANNA HARRISON and JOHN QUINCY ADAMS were half-20th cousins, once removed, or 21st cousins, once removed. Anna's paternal great(19)-grandfather, Richard De Clare (1130–76), was John's maternal great(20)-grandfather. Anna was descended through his son Roger "The Good" De Clare by his wife Alice De Meschines, while John was descended through his daughter Isabel De Clare (1171–1220) by his wife Eva MacMurrough (died in 1177).

ANNA HARRISON was BENJAMIN HARRISON'S grandmother through her son, John Scott Harrison.

ANNA HARRISON and GEORGE W. BUSH are 21st cousins, six times removed. Anna's paternal great(20)-grandparents, Ranulf III De Meschines (1070–1129) and Lucy Taillebois (1072–1136), were George's maternal great(26)-grandparents. Anna was descended through their daughter Alice De Meschines, while George is descended through their son Ranulf IV De Meschines.

JULIA TYLER and BENJAMIN HARRISON were sixth cousins, once removed. Julia's paternal great(5)-grandparents, William King (1595–1650) and Dorothy Hayne (born in 1601), were Benjamin's paternal great(6)-grandparents. Julia was descended through their son Samuel King, while Benjamin was descended through their daughter Deliverance King (1641–89).

JANE PIERCE and GEORGE W. BUSH are 12th cousins, nine times removed. Jane's paternal great(11)-grandparents, Maurice De Berkeley (1271–1326) and Eva La Zouche, were George's maternal great(20)-grandparents. Jane was descended through their son Thomas De Berkeley (1298–1368), while George is descended through their daughter Millicent De Berkeley.

JANE PIERCE and BARACK OBAMA are 16th cousins, seven times removed. Jane's paternal great(15)-grandparents, Humphrey de Bohun and Elizabeth Plantagenet, are Barack's maternal great(22)-grandparents. Jane is descended through their daughter Margaret, while Barack is descended through their son William.

MARY LINCOLN and JOHN QUINCY ADAMS were 14th cousins, twice removed. Mary's maternal great(15)-grandparents, John of Gaunt Beaufort (1340–98/9) and Catherine (or Katherine) Roet (1350–1403), were John's maternal great(13)-grandparents. Mary was descended through their son Sir John Beaufort (1371–1410), while John was descended through their son Henry Beaufort (1367–1447).

MARY LINCOLN and JAMES BUCHANAN were half-14th cousins, once removed, or 15th cousins, once removed. Mary's great(13)-grandfather, King Robert II of Scots, was James's paternal great(13)-grandfather. Mary was descended through his son John, who was later King Robert III. James was descended through his son Robert Stewart, Duke of Albany (1340–1420).

MARY LINCOLN and THEODORE ROOSEVELT were 10th cousins, three times removed. Mary's paternal great(9)-grandparents, Colin Campbell and Isabel Stewart, were Theodore's maternal great(12)-grandparents. Mary was descended through their daughter Helen Campbell, while Theodore was descended through their son Archibald Campbell.

MARY LINCOLN and GEORGE W. BUSH are fifth cousins, four times removed. Mary Lincoln's maternal great(4)-grandparents, John Peck (1640–91) and Mary Moss (1644–1725), are George's maternal great(8)-grandparents. Mary was descended through their daughter Elizabeth Peck (1673–1709), while George is descended through their son John Peck (1671–1768).

JULIA GRANT and JOHN QUINCY ADAMS were half-17th cousins, three times removed, or 18th cousins, three times removed. Julia's paternal great(19)-grandfather, King Edward I of England (1239–1307), was John's maternal great(16)-grandfather. Julia was descended through his son John De Botetorte (1265–1324) with his mistress Alice Lusignan, while John was descended through his daughter Elizabeth Plantagenet by his first wife, Eleanor de Castille (1241-90).

JULIA GRANT and BARACK OBAMA are 21st cousins, three times removed. Julia's paternal great(20)-grandparents, Sir William de Ros and Lucy FitzPiers, are Barack's maternal great(24)-grandparents. Julia was descended through their son Sir Robert de Ros, while Barack is descended through their son Sir William de Ros.

LUCY HAYES and FRANKLIN ROOSEVELT were seventh cousins. Lucy's maternal great(7)-grandparents, William Holton (died in 1691) and Mary, were Franklin's maternal great(7)-grandparents. Lucy was descended through their daughter Sarah, while Franklin was descended through their son William Jr.

LUCY HAYES and LYNDON JOHNSON were fourth cousins, three times removed. Lucy's paternal great(3)-grandparents, John William Webb (1649–94) and Mary Sanford (born in 1650), were Lyndon's paternal great(6)-grandparents. Lucy was descended through their son Giles Webb (1677–1732), while Lyndon was descended through their son John Webb, Jr. (1674–1721).

LUCRETIA GARFIELD and JOHN QUINCY ADAMS were 17th cousins, three times removed. Lucretia's great(19)-grandparents, King Edward I of England (1239–1307) and Eleanor de Castille (1241–90), were John's maternal great(16)-grandparents. Lucretia was descended through their daughter Joan Plantagenet (also known as Joan of Acre), while John was descended through their daughter Elizabeth Plantagenet.

LUCRETIA GARFIELD and GEORGE W. BUSH are 21st cousins, three times removed. Lucretia's maternal great(20)-grandparents, Roger De Quincy (1174–1264) and Helen of Galloway (also known as Helen McDonald), are George's maternal great(23)-grandparents. Lucretia was descended through their daughter Elizabeth De Quincy, while George is descended through their daughter Helen De Quincy.

LUCRETIA GARFIELD and BARACK OBAMA are 19th cousins, four times removed. Lucretia's maternal great(18)-grandparents, Humphrey de Bohun and Elizabeth Plantagenet, are Barack's maternal great(22)-grandparents. Lucretia was descended through their daughter Eleanor, while Barack is descended through their son William.

ELLEN ARTHUR and JOHN QUINCY ADAMS were 14th cousins. Ellen's great(13)-grandparents, John of Gaunt Beaufort (1340–98/9) and Catherine (or Katherine) Roet (1350–1403), were John's maternal great(13)-grandparents. Ellen was descended through their daughter Joan Beaufort (also known as Joan of Lancaster), while John was descended through their son Henry Beaufort (1367–1447).

ELLEN ARTHUR and BENJAMIN HARRISON were 23rd cousins, once removed. Ellen's paternal great(23)-grandparents, Ranulf III De Meschines (1070–1129) and Lucy Taillebois (1072–1136), were Benjamin's paternal great(22)-grandparents. Ellen was descended through their son Ranulf IV De Meschines, while Benjamin was descended through their daughter Alice De Meschines.

ELLEN ARTHUR and THEODORE ROOSEVELT were 14th cousins, once removed. Ellen's paternal great(13)-grandparents, John of Gaunt Beaufort (1340–98/9) and Katherine Roet (1350–1403), were Theodore's maternal great(14)-grandparents. Ellen was descended through their daughter Joan Beaufort (also known as Joan of Lancaster), while Theodore was descended through their son John Beaufort.

ELLEN ARTHUR and GEORGE W. BUSH are 21st cousins, twice removed. Ellen's great(20)-grandparents, William Marshall (1170–1219) and Isabel De Clare (1171–1220), are George's maternal great(22)-grandparents. Ellen was descended through their daughter Isabelle Marshall, while George is descended through their daughter Maud Marshall.

ELLEN ARTHUR and BARACK OBAMA are 18th cousins, six times removed. Ellen's paternal great(17)-grandparents, Sir William de Ros and Eustache FitzHugh, are Barack's maternal great(23)-grandparents. Ellen was descended through their daughter Lucy, while Barack is descended through their daughter Alice.

FRANCES CLEVELAND and RUTHERFORD HAYES were fourth cousins, twice removed. Frances's maternal great(5)-grandparents, Anthony Austin (1636–1708) and Esther Huggins (c1640–98), were Rutherford's maternal great(3)-grandparents. Frances was descended through their daughter

Esther Austin (born in 1686), while Rutherford was descended through their son Nathaniel Austin (1678–1760).

FRANCES CLEVELAND and FRANKLIN ROOSEVELT were sixth cousins, once removed. Frances's maternal great(6)-grandparents, Isaac Sheldon and Mary Woodford, were Franklin's maternal great(5)-grandparents. Frances was descended through their daughter Mary, while Franklin was descended through their son Thomas.

ALICE ROOSEVELT and BENJAMIN HARRISON were sixth cousins, three times removed. Alice's paternal great(8)-grandparents, Zachariah Symmes (1599–1671) and Sarah Baker (1605–73), were Benjamin's paternal great(5)-grandparents. Alice was descended through their daughter Mary Symmes, while Benjamin was descended through their son William Symmes (1626/28–1705).

ALICE ROOSEVELT and BARACK OBAMA are 22nd cousins, twice removed. Alice's paternal great(21)-grandparents, King Edward I of England (1239–1307) and Eleanor de Castille (1241–90), are Barack's maternal great(23)-grandparents. Alice was descended through their son King Edward II of England, while Barack is descended through their daughter Elizabeth Plantagenet.

EDITH ROOSEVELT and BENJAMIN HARRISON were seventh cousins, once removed. Edith's maternal great(7)-grandparents, Joseph Horton (1578–1640) and Mary Schuyler, were Benjamin's paternal great(6)-grandparents. Edith was descended through their son Thomas Horton (1596–1640), while Benjamin was descended through their son Barnabas Horton (1600–84).

EDITH ROOSEVELT and FRANKLIN ROOSEVELT were seventh cousins, once removed. Edith's maternal great(6)-grandparents, Robert Blott (died in 1665) and Susanna Selbee, were Franklin's maternal great(7)-grandparents. Edith was descended through their daughter Joanna, while Franklin was descended through their daughter Mary.

HELEN TAFT and BENJAMIN HARRISON were 23rd cousins, three times removed. Helen's maternal great(25)-grandparents, Ranulf III De Meschines (1070–1129) and Lucy Taillebois (1072–1136), were Benjamin's paternal great(22)-grandparents. Helen was descended through their son Ranulf IV De Meschines, while Benjamin was descended through their daughter Alice De Meschines.

HELEN TAFT and GEORGE W. BUSH are 23rd cousins, once removed. Helen's maternal great(22)-grandparents, William De Albini and Mabel De Meschines (born in 1123), are George's maternal great(23)-grandparents. Helen was descended through their daughter Nicole De Albini, while George is descended through their daughter Isabel De Albini.

HELEN TAFT and BARACK OBAMA are half-23rd cousins, three times removed, or 24th cousins, three times removed. Helen's maternal great(22)-grandfather, King John "Lackland" of England (died in 1216), is Barack's maternal great(25)-grandfather. Helen was descended through his illegitimate son Richard FitzRoy, while Barack is descended through his son King Henry III (1207–72).

ELLEN WILSON and JOHN QUINCY ADAMS were 17th cousins, four times removed. Ellen's paternal great(20)-grandparents, King Edward I of England (1239–1307) and Eleanor de Castille (1241–90), were John's maternal great(16)-grandparents. Ellen was descended through their daughter Joan Plantagenet (also known as Joan of Acre), while John was descended through their daughter Elizabeth Plantagenet.

ELLEN WILSON and FRANKLIN PIERCE were fifth cousins, twice removed. Ellen's maternal great(6)-grandparents, Daniel Brewer (1596–1646) and Joanna Morrill (1602–88), were Franklin's maternal great(4)-grandparents. Ellen was descended through their daughter Sarah Brewer (1638–1708), while Franklin was descended through their son Daniel Brewer (1624–1708).

ELLEN WILSON and ULYSSES GRANT were sixth cousins, once removed. Ellen's great(6)-grandparents, John Porter (1594–1648) and Anna White (1600–47), were Ulysses's paternal great(5)-grandparents. Ellen was descended through their daughter Ann or Anna (1621–53), while Ulysses was descended through their daughter Mary (1637–81).

ELLEN WILSON and RUTHERFORD HAYES were sixth cousins, once removed. Ellen's maternal great(6)-grandparents, Daniel Brewer (1596–1646) and Joanna Morrill (1602–88), were Rutherford's great(5)-grandparents. Ellen was descended through their daughter Sarah Brewer (1638–1708), while Rutherford was descended through their daughter Hannah Brewer (1630–1717).

ELLEN WILSON and GROVER CLEVELAND were seventh cousins. Ellen's great(6)-grandparents, John Porter (1594–1648) and Anna White (1600–47), were Grover's great(6)-grandparents. Ellen was descended through their daughter Ann or Anna (1621–53), while Grover was descended through their son Samuel (1635–89).

ELLEN WILSON and WARREN HARDING were eighth cousins. Ellen's maternal great(7)-grandparents, Robert Parke (1580–1644/5) and Martha Chaplin, were Warren's maternal great(7)-grandparents. Ellen was descended through their son William, while Warren was descended through their son Thomas.

ELLEN WILSON and GEORGE H.W. BUSH are sixth cousins, twice removed. Ellen's maternal great(5)-grandparents, John May (1631–71) and Sarah Brewer (1638–1708), were George's great(7)-grandparents. Ellen was descended through their daughter Sarah May, while George is descended through their great-granddaughter Elizabeth May (1730–89).

Therefore, ELLEN WILSON and GEORGE W. BUSH are sixth cousins, three times removed.

ELLEN WILSON and BARACK OBAMA are sixth cousins, five times removed. Ellen's paternal great(5)-grandparents, Edward FitzRandolph and Elizabeth Blossom, were Barack's maternal great(10)-grandparents. Ellen was descended through their son Benjamin, while Barack is descended through their son Nathaniel.

EDITH WILSON was THOMAS JEFFERSON'S great-great-niece. Edith's paternal great(3)-grandparents, Peter Jefferson (1708–57) and Jane Randolph (1720–76), were Thomas Jefferson's parents. Edith is descended through their daughter, Thomas's sister, Martha.

EDITH WILSON and JOHN QUINCY ADAMS were 14th cousins, twice removed. Edith's paternal great(15)-grandparents, John of Gaunt Beaufort (1340–98/9) and Catherine (or Katherine) Roet (1350–1403), were John's maternal great(13)-grandparents. Edith was descended through both their daughter Joan Beaufort and their son Sir John Beaufort (1371–1410), while John was descended through their son Henry Beaufort (1367–1447).

EDITH WILSON and JAMES BUCHANAN were 12th cousins, twice removed. Edith's great(11)-grandfather, King Robert II of Scots, was James's paternal great(13)-grandfather. Edith was descended through his daughter Catherine, while James was descended through his son Robert Stewart, Duke of Albany (1340–1420).

EDITH WILSON and THEODORE ROOSEVELT were 14th cousins, once removed. Edith's paternal great(14)-grandparents, Sir John Beaufort (1371–1410) and Margaret De Holland, were Theodore's maternal great(13)-grandparents. Edith was descended through their son Edmund Beaufort, while Theodore was descended through their daughter Joan Beaufort.

EDITH WILSON and BARACK OBAMA are 19th cousins, five times removed. Edith's paternal great(18)-grandparents, King Edward I of England (1239–1307) and Eleanor de Castille (1241–90), are Barack's maternal great(23)-grandparents. Edith is descended through their son King Edward II, while Barack is descended through their daughter Elizabeth Plantagenet.

FLORENCE HARDING and GEORGE W. BUSH are eighth cousins, three times removed. Florence's maternal great(7)-grandparents, Edward Marvin (1545–1615) and his wife Margaret, were George's maternal great(10)-grandparents. Florence was descended through their son Matthew Marvin (1600–78), while George is descended through their son Reinhold Marvin (1593–1662).

GRACE COOLIDGE and JOHN ADAMS were third cousins, four times removed. Grace's paternal great(6)-grandparents, William Cogswell (1619–1700) and Susanna Hawkes (1633–76), were John's maternal great-great-grandparents. Grace was descended through their son John Cogswell (1665–1710), while John was descended through their daughter Susanna Cogswell (1675–1701).

Therefore, GRACE COOLIDGE and JOHN QUINCY ADAMS were fourth cousins, three times removed.

GRACE COOLIDGE and her husband, CALVIN COOLIDGE, were eighth cousins, twice removed. Grace's paternal great(7)-grandparents, John Cogswell (died in 1669) and Elizabeth Thompson, were Calvin's paternal great(9)-grandparents. Grace was descended through their son William (1618/9–1700), while Calvin was descended through their daughter Hannah.

GRACE COOLIDGE and GEORGE W. BUSH are seventh cousins, three times removed. Grace's maternal great(6)-grandparents, Thomas Thayer (1596–1665) and Margery Wheeler (1597–1642), are George's maternal great(9)-grandparents. Grace was descended through their son Shadrack Thayer (1629–78), while George is descended through their son Fernando Thayer (1625–1713).

Lou Hoover and John Adams were third cousins, five times removed. Lou Hoover's maternal great(7)-grandparents, William Cogswell (1619–1700) and Susanna Hawkes (1633–76), were John Adams's maternal great-great-grandparents. Lou was descended through their daughter Hester Cogswell, while John was descended through their daughter Susanna Cogswell (1675–1701).

Therefore, Lou Hoover and John Quincy Adams were fourth cousins, four times removed.

Lou Hoover and James Garfield were sixth cousins, three times removed. Lou's maternal great(8)-grandparents, Nicholas Danforth and Elizabeth Symmes, were James's paternal great(5)-grandparents. Lou was descended through their daughter Mary Danforth, while James was descended through their daughter Anne Danforth.

Lou Hoover and Calvin Coolidge were ninth cousins, once removed. Lou's maternal great(8)-grandparents, John Cogswell (died in 1669) and Elizabeth Thompson, were Calvin's paternal great(9)-grandparents. Lou was descended through their son William (1618/9–1700), while Calvin was descended through their daughter Hannah.

Eleanor Roosevelt and John Quincy Adams were 14th cousins, twice removed. Eleanor's paternal great(15)-grandparents, John of Gaunt Beaufort (1340–98/9) and Catherine (or Katherine) Roet (1350–1403), were John's maternal great(13)-grandparents. Eleanor was descended from their son Sir John Beaufort (1371–1410), while John was descended through their son Henry Beaufort (1367–1447).

Eleanor Roosevelt and Martin Van Buren were third cousins, four times removed. Eleanor's great(6)-grandparents, Lucas Wyndgard and Anna Van Hoesen, were Martin's maternal great-great-grandparents. Eleanor was descended through their daughter Margaret Lucasse Wyndgard, while Martin was descended through their daughter Elizabeth Lucasse Wyndgard.

ELEANOR ROOSEVELT was THEODORE ROOSEVELT'S niece. Her father was his younger brother, Elliott (1860–94).

ELEANOR ROOSEVELT and her husband, FRANKLIN DELANO ROOSEVELT, were fifth cousins, once removed. Eleanor's paternal great(5)-grandparents, Nicholas Roosevelt (1658–1742) and Heyltje Jans Knust, were Franklin's paternal great(4)-grandparents. Eleanor was descended through their son Johannes (born in 1689), while Franklin was descended through their son Jacobus (1692–1776).

ELEANOR ROOSEVELT and BARACK OBAMA are 18th cousins, five times removed. Eleanor's maternal great(17)-grandparents, Humphrey de Bohun and Elizabeth Plantagenet, are Barack's maternal great(22)-grandparents. Eleanor was descended through their daughter Margaret, while Barack is descended through their son William.

BESS TRUMAN and RUTHERFORD HAYES were half-seventh cousins, three times removed. Bess's paternal great(8)-grandmother, Elizabeth Charde (died in 1643), was Rutherford's maternal great(6)-grandmother. Bess was descended through her daughter Abigail (with her second husband, Thomas Ford, who died in 1676), while Rutherford was descended through her son Aaron Jr. (with her first husband, Aaron Cooke, who died in 1615).

BESS TRUMAN and GROVER CLEVELAND were half-eighth cousins, twice removed. Bess's paternal great(8)-grandmother Elizabeth Charde (died in 1643) was Grover's paternal great(7)-grandmother. Bess was descended through her daughter Abigail (with her second husband, Thomas Ford, who died in 1676), while Grover was descended through her son Aaron Jr. (with her first husband, Aaron Cooke, who died in 1615).

BESS TRUMAN and BENJAMIN HARRISON were 12th cousins, four times removed. Bess's maternal great(15)-grandparents, John Fortescue (1420–80) and Jane Preston, were Benjamin's paternal great(11)-grandparents.

Bess was descended through their son William Fortescue, while Benjamin was descended through their daughter Joan Fortescue.

BESS TRUMAN and FRANKLIN ROOSEVELT were seventh cousins, once removed. Bess's paternal great(7)-grandparents, John Strong (died in 1699) and Abigail Ford, were Franklin's maternal great(6)-grandparents. Bess was descended through their daughters Mary and Elizabeth (whose son Ebenezer and daughter Abigail married), while Franklin was descended through their son Ebenezer.

They were also sixth cousins, twice removed, through Isaac Sheldon and Mary Woodford: Bess's maternal great(7)-grandparents and Franklin's maternal great(5)-grandparents. Bess was descended through their daughter Mindwell, while Franklin was descended through their son Thomas.

BESS TRUMAN and BARACK OBAMA are half 28th cousins, once removed, or 29th cousins, once removed. Bess's maternal great(27)-grandfather, King Henry I of England (1068–1135), is Barack's maternal great(28)-grandfather. Bess was descended through his illegitimate son Robert of Caen, while Barack is descended through his daughter Queen Matilda I (1102–67).

MAMIE EISENHOWER and JOHN ADAMS were fourth cousins, five times removed. Mamie's paternal great(8)-grandparents, John Cogswell (died in 1669) and Elizabeth Thompson, were John's maternal great(3)-grandparents. Mamie was descended through their daughter Hannah, while John was descended through their son William (1618/9–1700).

Therefore, MAMIE EISENHOWER and JOHN QUINCY ADAMS were fifth cousins, four times removed.

MAMIE EISENHOWER and THEODORE ROOSEVELT were 14th cousins, four times removed. Mamie's paternal great(17)-grandparents, Sir John Beaufort (1371–1410) and Margaret De Holland, were Theodore's maternal great(13)-grandparents. Mamie was descended through their son Edmund Beaufort, while Theodore was descended through their daughter Joan Beaufort.

MAMIE EISENHOWER and CALVIN COOLIDGE were eighth cousins. Mamie's paternal great(7)-grandparents, Cornelius Waldo and Hannah Cogswell, were Calvin's paternal great(8)-grandparents. Mamie was descended through their son John, while Calvin was descended through their son Daniel.

MAMIE EISENHOWER and BARACK OBAMA are 19th cousins, once removed. Mamie's paternal great(18)-grandparents, Richard FitzAlan and Elizabeth de Bohun, are Barack's maternal great(20)-grandparents. Mamie was descended through their daughter Joan, while Barack is descended through their daughter Elizabeth.

LADY BIRD JOHNSON and JOHN TYLER were half-fourth cousins, five times removed. Lady Bird's great(8)-grandfather, Walter Chiles III (died in 1671) married, as his second wife, Susanna Brooks. Lady Bird is descended through their son Henry Chiles (1669–1719/20). Walter III's first wife, Mary Page, was John's paternal great(3)-grandmother. John was descended through their daughter Elizabeth Chiles.

JANE WYMAN (REAGAN) and BENJAMIN HARRISON were fourth cousins, three times removed. Jane's maternal great(6)-grandparents, Caleb Horton (1687–1722) and Phebe Terry (1690–1776), were Benjamin's paternal great(3)-grandparents. Jane was descended through their son Nathaniel Horton (1719–1804), while Benjamin was descended through their daughter Phoebe Horton (1722–93).

NANCY REAGAN and FRANKLIN ROOSEVELT are sixth cousins, three times removed. Nancy's paternal great(8)-grandparents, Isaac Sheldon and Mary Woodford, were Franklin's maternal great(5)-grandparents. Nancy is descended through their daughter Ruth, while Franklin was descended through their son Thomas.

NANCY REAGAN and GEORGE W. BUSH are 21st cousins, once removed. Nancy's paternal great(20)-grandparents, Eudes La Zouche and Millicent

De Cantelupe, were George's maternal great(21)-grandparents. Nancy is descended through their daughter Elizabeth La Zouche, while George is descended through their daughter Eva La Zouche.

NANCY REAGAN and BARACK OBAMA are half 28th cousins, once removed, or 29th cousins, once removed. Nancy's paternal great(27)-grandfather, King Henry I of England (1068–1135), is Barack's maternal great(28)-grandparents. Nancy is descended through his illegitimate son Robert of Caen, while Barack is descended through his daughter Queen Matilda I (1102–67).

BARBARA BUSH and JOHN QUINCY ADAMS are 20th cousins, twice removed. Barbara's great(21)-grandparents, William Marshall (1170–1219) and Isabel De Clare (1171–1220), were John's maternal great(19)-grandparents. Barbara is descended through their daughter Maud Marshall, while John was descended through their daughter Eva Marshall.

BARBARA BUSH and FRANKLIN PIERCE are fourth cousins, four times removed. Barbara's paternal great(7)-grandparents, Thomas Pierce (1618–83) and Elizabeth Cole (1614–88), were Franklin's paternal great(3)-grandparents. Barbara is descended through their son James Pierce (1659–1742), while Franklin is descended through their son Stephen Pierce (1651–1733).

Barbara and Franklin are also second cousins, five times removed. Barbara's paternal great(6)-grandparents, Stephen Pierce (1679–1749) and Esther Fletcher (1681–1741/2), were Franklin's great-grandparents. Franklin was descended through their son Benjamin Pierce (1726–64), while Barbara is descended through their daughter Esther Pierce (born in 1711).

Some confusion arises here, because Esther Pierce's daughter Esther Richardson (1727–1819) married James Pierce's (1659–1742) grandson Joshua Pierce (1722–71) in 1753, reuniting two branches with the marriage of second cousins, once removed.

BARBARA BUSH and JAMES GARFIELD are fifth cousins, four times removed. Barbara's paternal great(8)-grandparents, Walter Cook (died in 1695 or 1696) and his wife Catharine (died in 1695), were James's maternal great(4)-grandparents. Barbara is descended through their son John Cook (1653–1718), while James was descended through their son Nicholas Cook (1660–1730).

BARBARA BUSH and BENJAMIN HARRISON are 23rd cousins, three times removed. Barbara's paternal great(25)-grandparents, Ranulf III De Meschines (1070–1129) and Lucy Taillebois (1072–1136), were Benjamin's paternal great(22)-grandparents. Barbara is descended through their son Ranulf IV De Meschines, while Benjamin was descended through their daughter Alice De Meschines.

BARBARA BUSH and WILLIAM TAFT are fifth cousins, three times removed. Barbara's paternal great(7)-grandparents, Peter Holbrook and Alice Godfrey, were William's maternal great(4)-grandparents. Barbara is descended through their son Silvanus Holbrook, while William was descended through their son William Holbrook (1693–c1776).

BARBARA BUSH is GEORGE W. BUSH's mother.

45. Eisenhower and Nixon, the Only Marriage Uniting Two Presidential Families

Most Presidential families are related through shared ancestors. Some of those families are related very closely, others more distantly. On the close side, there were the Adamses (father and son), the Bushes after them, the Harrisons (grandfather and grandson), and James Madison and Zachary Taylor (who were second cousins). At the other end of the spectrum, there were 22nd cousins John Quincy Adams and Benjamin Harrison (related through Richard De Clare, who lived from 1130 to 1176), and 20th cousins John Quincy Adams and George W. Bush (related through William Marshall (1170–1219) and Isabel De Clare (1171–1220)).

But so far as we know, there has only been one joining of Presidential descendants.

Julie Nixon met David Eisenhower at the 1956 Republican National Convention. They may have met earlier, but this event was definite. At the time, the two eight-year-olds were the youngest generation of the respective political families. He was the only grandson of President Dwight Eisenhower, who was being nominated for reelection. She was the younger daughter of Vice President Richard Nixon.

At the following inaugural festivities, a picture of the two looking at each other was snapped, which has become famous. Were they plotting their far-future wedding at that early date? Had two political powerhouses already decided to an alliance of marriage? Most probably, there was no grand conspiracy: Julie had a black eye from a recent sledding accident, and the President suggested she hide it for the photo by turning her head. Simultaneously, David was looking to his left, and history was made.

In actuality, the two met only a few times as children, although the *Washington Post* noted each "had a mother who was forever saying 'I want my child to have a normal life'—while normal mothers were talking about their children growing up to be president."

Julie Nixon was born on July 5, 1948, while her father was serving his first term as a member of the House of Representatives. Her older sister, Tricia, had been born in February 1946.

Dwight David Eisenhower II (known as David) was born on March 31, 1948, in West Point, New York, where his father, John Eisenhower, was serving at the US Military Academy. John was the son of General Dwight Eisenhower, who had just finished his stint as Army Chief of Staff, and had then taken up the reins as the President of Columbia University.

In the fall of 1966, David was a freshman at Amherst, while Julie was at Smith. Both were invited to address the Republican Women's Club of Hadley, Massachusetts, and they jointly decided to decline the offer. But soon after that, David and his roommate visited Smith to take Julie and a friend out for ice cream. "I was broke," David later said. "My roommate forgot his wallet. The girls paid."

In November, they watched the midterm election returns together, and in December, he escorted her to her debutante ball. This public appearance made headlines for the scions of the two retired political families. A year later, Julie Nixon and Dwight David Eisenhower II were engaged.

The romance was nothing but good news for Richard Nixon, who was at the time attempting a unique political comeback, campaigning for the Republican nomination for President. He could now be the proud father, joining his family with what was still the most popular brand name in American politics. *Time* magazine opined, "In a year of wee-hour skull sessions, G.O.P. strategists could hardly have cooked up such a promotional coup. The idea would have seemed too stagy or cloyingly obvious: the candidate's perky, pretty 20-year-old daughter Julie becoming engaged to the 20-year-old grandson of Dwight Eisenhower on the very eve of the presidential primary race." The *New York Times* continued, "In the realm of national politics, nothing like it has been seen since the marriage of

Alice Roosevelt, daughter of President Theodore Roosevelt, and Nicholas Longworth, then Speaker of the House."

In the summer of 1968, David was a star campaign attraction. "I always campaign better with an Eisenhower," Nixon would joke as he introduced David to appreciative crowds. *Time* emphasized David's appeal: "Inheriting both the name and his grandfather's magnificent grin, the tousled, some-times diffident college junior lends a certain symmetry to the Nixon drive in the minds of many Republicans. His very presence recalls calmer times when Ike was in the White House."

But politics was not the entirety of David and Julie's relationship: they could have had a White House wedding, but Julie wanted something more private. She said that she and David were historic enough without having their wedding in the East Room and instead chose Marble Collegiate Church in Manhattan. They also stuck with their planned wedding date of December 22, 1968, a month before Nixon's inauguration.

In late 1968, Ike was in Walter Reed Army Medical Center, recovering from his fourth heart attack (though he would never fully recover; he died there in March 1969), so Nixon took the family festivities to him, celebrating Thanksgiving at the hospital. Ike and Mamie were unable to attend the wedding, so NBC tried (unsuccessfully) to get them a closed-circuit view of the festivities. The church, however, was packed with friends, family, and politicians, including incoming Cabinet members, and former New York governor Thomas Dewey, who was asked a poser by an usher: which side he was with? Eventually, he said "both!" and the usher led him to the Nixon side.

After David and Julie graduated from college, she became active as a spokesperson for children's issues, the environment, and the elderly. She gave tours of the White House to disabled children and filled in for her mother at events. From 1973 to 1975, she was the Assistant Managing Editor of the *Saturday Evening Post* and helped establish Curtis Publishing's book division.

David served in the Naval Reserve for three years and then went on to earn his JD in 1976.

David and Julie have three children: actress Jennie Elizabeth (born in 1978), Alexander "Alex" Richard (1980), and Melanie Catherine (1984). They also have three grandchildren. These six offspring are the only people to have ancestors in both their maternal and paternal lines who were President of the United States.

David is an author and a professor and public policy fellow at the University of Pennsylvania. He was a finalist for the Pulitzer Prize in history in 1987 for *Eisenhower: At War, 1943–1945*.

Julie is the author of several books, including *Eye on Nixon: A Photographic Study of the President and the Man*, *Julie Eisenhower's Cookbook for Children*, *Special People* (essays on famous people from history), and *Pat Nixon: The Untold Story*.

In 2010, Julie and David co-authored *Going Home to Glory: A Memoir of Life with Dwight D. Eisenhower, 1961–1969*.

In a 2015 interview, David's three younger sisters commented on the relationship between Ike and Nixon. They said the two had a good working relationship, but at the moment of Julie and David's wedding, they became family, in deed as well as name.

46. The First Ladies Who Had All Their Children Live to See Them Become First Ladies

ABIGAIL FILLMORE (1850–53) was the first First Lady to have all her children live to see her become First Lady. Her son, Millard Powers Fillmore, was born in 1828 and died in 1889. Her daughter, Mary Abigail Fillmore, was born in 1832 and died of cholera in 1854.

JULIA GRANT (1869–77). Four children: Frederick Dent Grant (1850–1912), Ulysses S. Grant, Jr. (1852–1929), Ellen "Nellie" Wrenshall Grant Sartoris Jones (1855–1922), and Jesse Root Grant (1858–1934).

FRANCES CLEVELAND (1886–89, 93–97) did not have any of her children die before taking office, but then again, she married Grover in 1886, after he took office in 1885. They had one child between his two terms (Ruth, 1891–1904), two children during his second term (Esther, 1893–1980; and Marion, 1895–1977), and two children after he retired (Richard, 1897–1974; and Francis, 1903–95).

EDITH ROOSEVELT (1901–09). Five children: Theodore Roosevelt, Jr. (1887–1944), Kermit Roosevelt (1889–1943), Ethel Carow Roosevelt (1891–1977), Archibald Bulloch Roosevelt (1894–1979), and Quentin Roosevelt (1897–1918). She also had one stepdaughter, Alice Lee Roosevelt Longworth (1884–1980), who was Theodore's daughter with his first wife.

HELEN TAFT (1909–13). Three children: Robert Alphonso Taft (1889–1953), Helen Herron Taft Manning (1891–1987), and Charles Phelps Taft II (1897–1983).

ELLEN WILSON (1913–14). Three children: Margaret Woodrow Wilson (1886–1944), Jessie Woodrow Wilson Sayre (1887–1933), and Eleanor Randolph Wilson McAdoo (1889–1967).

GRACE COOLIDGE (1923–29). Two sons: John Coolidge (1906–2000) and Calvin Coolidge (1908–24).

LOU HOOVER (1929–33). Two sons: Herbert Charles Hoover (1903–69) and Allan Henry Hoover (1907–93).

BESS TRUMAN (1945–53). One daughter: (Mary) Margaret Truman Daniel (born in 1924).

LADY BIRD JOHNSON (1963–69). Two daughters: Lynda Bird Johnson Robb (born in 1944) and Luci Baines Johnson Nugent (born in 1947).

PAT NIXON (1969–74). Two daughters: Patricia Nixon Cox (born in 1946) and Julie Nixon Eisenhower (born in 1948).

BETTY FORD (1974–77). Four children: Michael Gerald Ford (born in 1950), John "Jack" Gardner Ford (born in 1952), Steven Meigs Ford (born in 1956), and Susan Elizabeth Ford (born in 1957).

ROSALYNN CARTER (1977–81). Four children: John "Jack" William Carter (born in 1947), James Earl "Chip" Carter III (born in 1950), (Donnell) Jeffrey Carter (born in 1952), and Amy Lynn Carter (born in 1967).

HILLARY CLINTON (1993–2001). One daughter: Chelsea Victoria (born in 1980).

LAURA BUSH (2001–09). Two daughters: twins Barbara and Jenna (born in 1981).

MICHELLE OBAMA (2009–). Two daughters: Malia (born in 1998) and Sasha (born in 2001).

47. The First Ladies Who Had All Their Siblings Live to See Them Become First Ladies

IDA SAXTON MCKINLEY (1897–1901): Mary (1848–1917) and George (1849–98). Her brother George was murdered on October 7, 1898.

BESS WALLACE TRUMAN (1945–53): Frank (1887–1960), George (1892–1963), and David (1900–57).

JACQUELINE BOUVIER KENNEDY (1961–63): Caroline Lee (born in 1933).

ROSALYNN SMITH CARTER (1977–81): Murray (1929–2003), Jerrold (1932–2003), and Lillian (born in 1936).

NANCY DAVIS REAGAN (1981–89): She has no siblings, but one stepbrother, Richard Davis (born in 1927).

BARBARA PIERCE BUSH (1989–93): Martha (1920–99), James (1921–93), and Scott (born in 1930).

HILLARY RODHAM CLINTON (1993–2001): Hugh (born in 1950) and Anthony (born in 1954).

MICHELLE ROBINSON OBAMA (2009–): Craig (born in 1962).

48. *The First Ladies Who Gave Birth to Children after Leaving Office*

1. JULIA GARDINER TYLER (1820–89) was the first woman to marry a sitting President. She married John Tyler (whose first wife, Letitia, died in 1842) on June 26, 1844. Julia was 30 years younger than her husband. After leaving office in 1845, Julia and John retired to his Virginia plantation and had seven children between 1846 and 1860: David Gardiner (1846–1927), who was a Congressman from 1893 to 1897; John Alexander (1848–83); Julia Gardiner (1849–71); Lachlan (1851–1902); Lyon Gardiner (1853–1935), who was President of William and Mary College from 1888 to 1919; Robert FitzWalter (1856–1927); and Pearl (1860–1947). John, a southerner, died in 1862. He supported the South in its conflict with the North, called for Virginia's secession, and was elected to the Provisional Congress of the Confederacy before his death. Julia, a northerner by birth, adopted her husband's views, and though she was a supporter of the South, she returned to her family home in New York following John's death. These views caused strained relations with her family, and she returned to Virginia a few years before her death, where she lived out her final years with the aid of her grown children.

Like his father, Lyon Gardiner Tyler married twice and had children with both wives. Some of his children came along quite late in his life. Following his first wife's death in 1921, he married Sue Ruffin, with whom he had three children: Lyon Gardiner Tyler, Jr. (born 1924), Harrison Ruffin Tyler (born 1928), and Henry Tyler, who died in infancy. As of this writing, Lyon Jr. and Harrison both survive, making their grandfather the earliest President with living grandchildren.

2. FRANCES FOLSOM CLEVELAND (1864–1947) was Grover Cleveland's ward and then his wife. They married on June 2, 1886, during Cleveland's first term as President. Her first child, Ruth, was born in 1891, between the

Clevelands' two non-consecutive terms in the White House (she died of diphtheria in 1904). Esther (1893–1980) was the only Presidential child born in the White House. Marion (1895–1977) was born in Massachusetts during her father's second term. Richard Folsom (1897–1974) was a Marine officer during World War I and then graduated from Harvard Law School. Francis Grover (1903–95) graduated from Harvard and was an actor. Grover died in 1908, and Frances became the first Presidential widow to remarry in 1913, when she married Thomas J. Preston, a Princeton professor of archaeology.

3. MARY SCOTT LORD DIMMICK HARRISON (1858–1948) was the niece of Benjamin Harrison's first wife, Caroline. During her aunt's final illness, Mary served as White House hostess for her uncle. Caroline died in October 1892, days before her husband lost his bid for reelection to the Presidency. After Benjamin retired from office, he and Mary fell in love, and they married on April 6, 1896. His two grown children (born in 1854 and 1858) objected to the marriage, but Harrison's former Vice President and several of his Cabinet officers attended the wedding. The retired President and the second Mrs. Harrison had one child, Elizabeth (1897–1955), who graduated from New York University Law School in 1919 and married James Blaine Walker in 1922. Walker was the grandnephew of her father's Secretary of State, James G. Blaine. Benjamin died in 1901 and was buried in Indianapolis. When Mary died 47 years later, she was buried next to her President-husband.

49. The First Ladies Who Were

49a. Firstborn Children

Eleven of the First Ladies were firstborns.

MARTHA DANDRIDGE CUSTIS WASHINGTON had three younger brothers and five younger sisters.

MARTHA WAYLES SKELTON JEFFERSON had three younger half-brothers and seven younger half-sisters.

LUCRETIA RUDOLPH GARFIELD had two younger brothers and one younger sister.

FRANCES FOLSOM CLEVELAND had one younger sister, who was born in 1871 and died the next year.

IDA SAXTON MCKINLEY had two younger siblings: Mary (1848–1917) and George (1849–98).

ELLEN AXSON WILSON had two younger brothers and one younger sister.

ELEANOR ROOSEVELT had two younger siblings: Elliott (1889–93) and (Gracie) Hall (1891–1941).

BESS WALLACE TRUMAN had three younger brothers: Frank (1887–1960), George (1892–1963), and David (1900–57).

JACQUELINE BOUVIER KENNEDY had one younger sister: Caroline Lee (born in 1933).

ROSALYNN SMITH CARTER had three younger siblings: Murray (1929–2003), Jerrold (1932–2003), and Lillian (1936–).

HILLARY RODHAM CLINTON has two younger brothers: Hugh (born in 1950) and Anthony (born in 1954).

49b. Lastborn Children

Six of the First Ladies were lastborns.

ANNA SYMMES HARRISON had one older sister.
MARGARET SMITH TAYLOR had three older brothers and three older sisters.
LADY BIRD TAYLOR JOHNSON had two older brothers.
PAT RYAN NIXON had two older brothers, two older half-brothers, and two
    older half-sisters.
BETTY BLOOMER FORD had two older brothers.
MICHELLE LAVAUGHN ROBINSON OBAMA has one older brother.

49c. Only Children

Five of the First Ladies were only children (none of the Presidents were):
ELIZA MCCARDLE JOHNSON, ELLEN HERNDON ARTHUR, GRACE GOODHUE
COOLIDGE, NANCY DAVIS REAGAN, and LAURA WELCH BUSH.

49d. Not Quites

NANCY DAVIS REAGAN had no siblings, but her adoptive father (her mother's second husband), Loyal Davis, had a son from his previous marriage, Nancy's stepbrother, Richard Davis (born in 1927).

49e. Unknowns

Several of the First Ladies' families are not exactly known, in terms of either the number of siblings or the birth order. What we do know about them is that:

ELIZABETH KORTRIGHT MONROE had one brother and three sisters.
HANNAH HOES VAN BUREN had one brother and one sister.

LETITIA CHRISTIAN TYLER had three brothers and three sisters.

JULIA GARDINER TYLER had two brothers and one sister.

JANE APPLETON PIERCE had three brothers and two sisters.

JULIA GRANT had four brothers and three sisters.

LUCY WEBB HAYES had two brothers.

CAROLINE SCOTT HARRISON had two brothers and two sisters.

EDITH CAROW ROOSEVELT had one sister.

FLORENCE KLING HARDING had two brothers.

LOU HENRY HOOVER had one sister.

50. First Ladies' Fathers' Occupations

Many of the First Ladies' fathers had multiple occupations during their lifetimes. When the nation was founded, it was an agrarian society with the upper class also serving in public offices of one sort or another, so those two categories are no real surprise.

1. FARMER/PLANTER/LANDOWNER. Just as on the Presidents' list, the greatest number of First Ladies had fathers who worked the land in one way or another, although the number is far fewer for First Ladies: only eleven. The list of First Ladies with farming fathers is: Washington, Jefferson, Madison, Anna Harrison, Letitia Tyler, Julia Tyler, Polk, Taylor, Grant, Garfield, and Lady Bird Johnson.

2. MERCHANTS—third on the Presidential list—fathered nine First Ladies: Monroe, Louisa Adams, Polk, Grant, Edith Roosevelt, Eisenhower, Lady Bird Johnson, Ford, and Nancy Reagan.

3. PUBLIC OFFICIAL. Seven men who fathered First Ladies served in some sort of public office, though as yet, no Presidents, Governors, or Congressmen have had daughters who married Presidents. The First Ladies who had public-official fathers were: Jackson, Anna Harrison, Julia Tyler, Taft, Edith Wilson, Truman, and Jane Wyman-Reagan.

4 (tie). RELIGIOUS CAREERS OR MINISTRIES. Five fathers of First Ladies had religious careers or ministries: Abigail Adams, Abigail Fillmore, Pierce, Caroline Harrison, and Ellen Wilson.

4 (tie). MILITARY. Five fathers of First Ladies served in the military: Monroe, Jackson, Letitia Tyler, Taylor, and Grant.

4 (tie). BANKER. Five fathers of First Ladies had banking careers: Lincoln, McKinley, Alice Roosevelt, Harding, and Hoover.

First Ladies' mothers, on the other hand, were by and large homemakers, housewives, or otherwise occupied with caring for their families. The only mothers known to have had jobs outside the home were Michelle Obama and Jane Wyman's mothers (who were secretaries), Laura Bush's mother (a bookkeeper in her husband's business), Nancy Reagan's mother (an actress), and Rosalynn Carter's mother (a dressmaker).

OTHER FAMILY MEMBERS

51. The Senior Presidential Child

The 43 men who have been President have fathered an acknowledged 158 children—89 boys and 69 girls (not counting stepchildren or adopted children, although the list does include Warren Harding's illegitimate daughter by Nan Britton)—of whom 123 lived to adulthood. At least 96 Presidential children had children of their own, making the 43 Presidents responsible for at least 335 grandchildren. The "average" President would have 2.1 sons, 1.6 daughters, and 8 grandchildren.

George Washington had no children of his own, but his two stepchildren (wife Martha's younger children from a previous marriage), John and Martha, died in 1781 and 1773 and were thus never Presidential children. The first President to have living children during his term of office was John Adams. His first child, daughter Abigail Adams Smith, was thus the first Senior Presidential Child. She held that position from her father's inauguration, on March 4, 1797, until her death from cancer on August 15, 1813.

Abigail was followed by her brother, John Quincy, who was the Senior Presidential Child for 34 years, 192 days (the longest tenure of any). He was also President from 1825 to 1829, the only person to have both titles ever, let alone simultaneously. George W. Bush (President from 2001 to 2009 and the oldest son of President George H.W. Bush) may one day be the Senior Presidential Child (although the current Senior Presidential Child, Caroline Kennedy, is 11 years younger than he is).

The person to hold the title for the shortest length of time was James Rudolph Garfield, whose father had been President in 1881. He took the title on March 18, 1950, when Fanny Hayes Smith (Rutherford Hayes's daughter) died. Garfield died six days later and was succeeded by his brother Irvin.

Only 19 people have been the Senior Presidential Child, and only 12 Presidents have been the father of the Senior Presidential Child.

The Senior Presidential Child

Name	Father (and his term of office)	Date of title (and predecessor's death)
Abigail Adams Smith	John Adams (1797–1801)	no predecessor
President John Quincy Adams	John Adams (1797–1801)	August 15, 1813
John Payne Todd (stepson)	James Madison (1809–17)	February 23, 1848
Charles Francis Adams, Sr.	John Quincy Adams (1825–29)	1852
John Tyler, Jr.	John Tyler (1841–45)	November 21, 1886
Letitia Tyler Semple	John Tyler (1841–45)	January 26, 1896
David Gardiner Tyler	John Tyler (born after his father left office in 1845)	December 28, 1907
Lyon Gardiner Tyler	John Tyler (born after his father left office in 1845)	September 5, 1927
Pearl Tyler Ellis	John Tyler (born after her father left office in 1845)	February 12, 1935
Fanny Hayes Smith	Rutherford Hayes (1877–81)	June 30, 1947
James Rudolph Garfield	James A. Garfield (1881)	March 18, 1950
Irvin McDowell Garfield	James A. Garfield (1881)	March 24, 1950
Abram Garfield	James A. Garfield (1881)	July 18, 1951
Esther Cleveland Bosanquet	Grover Cleveland (1885–89, 1893–97; born during her father's second term)	October 16, 1958
Helen Herron Taft Manning	William Taft (1909–13)	June 26, 1980

Elizabeth Ann Britton (illegitimate)	Warren Harding (1921–23)	February 21, 1987
Margaret Truman Daniel	Harry Truman (1945–53)	November 17, 2005
John Sheldon Doud Eisenhower	Dwight Eisenhower (1953–61)	January 29, 2008
Caroline Bouvier Kennedy Schlossberg	John Kennedy (1961–63)	December 21, 2013

The next most senior Presidential child is Lyndon Johnson's elder daughter, Lynda Bird Johnson Robb, who is 13 years older than Caroline Kennedy and is the oldest living Presidential child.

52. The Longest-Lived Presidential Children

Four of the 43 Presidents have lived at least 90 years, and four of the 49 Presidential wives have exceeded that mark, which is why it's surprising that, thus far, only five of the more than 160 Presidential children have lived so long.

1. ALICE LEE ROOSEVELT LONGWORTH. Born February 12, 1884, she was the only child of Theodore Roosevelt's first wife, Alice, who died two days after her birth, at the age of 22. A very public person herself, the younger Alice married Ohio Representative Nicholas Longworth (who was later Speaker of the House) in the East Room of the White House in 1906. She died February 20, 1980, eight days after her 96th birthday.

2. HELEN HERRON TAFT MANNING. Born August 1, 1891, she was the second of William Howard Taft's three children. She earned a doctorate in history from Yale and was later Dean of Bryn Mawr College. She died February 21, 1987, aged 95 years, 204 days.

3. JOHN COOLIDGE. Born September 7, 1906, he was Calvin Coolidge's first son. He was a railroad and printing executive, and his wife's father was Governor of Connecticut. He died May 31, 2000, aged 93 years, 266 days.

4. FRANCIS GROVER CLEVELAND. Born July 18, 1903, six years after his father left office for the second time, he was the youngest of the Cleveland children. He graduated from Harvard and was an actor. He died on November 8, 1995, aged 92 years, 113 days, more than 158 years after his father was born.

5. JOHN SHELDON DOUD EISENHOWER. Born August 3, 1922, he was Dwight Eisenhower's only child to live to adulthood. He, too, graduated from

West Point, retired from active duty in the Army as a Lieutenant Colonel, and from the Army Reserve as a General. He served as US Ambassador to Belgium from 1969 to 1971, and died on December 21, 2013, aged 91 years, 140 days.

6. PEARL TYLER ELLIS. Born June 20, 1860, more than 15 years after her father, John Tyler, retired from the Presidency and less than two years before his death, she was the last child of his second wife, Julia Gardiner. Pearl died more than 157 years after her father was born, on June 30, 1947, aged 87 years, 10 days.

The oldest living Presidential child is Lyndon Johnson's elder daughter, Lynda Bird Johnson Robb, who was born March 19, 1944.

Only nine other Presidential children lived at least 85 years:

LETITIA TYLER SEMPLE (JOHN TYLER'S daughter with his first wife): born May 11, 1821, died December 28, 1907, aged 86 years, 231 days.

MARY ELIZABETH TAYLOR BLISS DANDRIDGE (ZACHARY TAYLOR'S daughter): born April 20, 1824, died July 26, 1909, aged 85 years, 117 days.

ABRAM GARFIELD (JAMES GARFIELD'S son): born November 21, 1872, died October 16, 1958, aged 85 years, 329 days.

ESTHER CLEVELAND BOSANQUET (GROVER CLEVELAND'S daughter): born September 9, 1893, died June 26, 1980, aged 86 years, 290 days.

ETHEL CAROW ROOSEVELT DERBY (THEODORE ROOSEVELT'S daughter): born August 13, 1891, died December 10, 1977, aged 86 years, 119 days.

ARCHIBALD BULLOCH ROOSEVELT (THEODORE ROOSEVELT'S son): born April 9, 1894, died October 13, 1979, aged 85 years, 187 days.

CHARLES PHELPS TAFT II (WILLIAM TAFT'S son): born September 20, 1897, died June 24, 1983, aged 85 years, 277 days.

ELIZABETH ANN BRITTON (WARREN HARDING'S illegitimate daughter): born October 22, 1919, died November 17, 2005, aged 86 years, 26 days.

ALLAN HENRY HOOVER (HERBERT HOOVER'S son): born July 17, 1907, died November 4, 1993, aged 86 years, 110 days.

53. White House Weddings

When the White House was first built, it was the poor American cousin of European palaces: a temporary residence for the President and his family, along with office space and some rooms for public events. A decade and a half after John Adams became the first President to live in it, the British burned it during the War of 1812. But it was rebuilt, expanded, and over the years became more than a building: it became a symbol. It has served more than two centuries as both an office building and a temporary residence for the President of the United States and his family. The White House became so iconic that when it had to be torn down and rebuilt (1949–52), the exterior shell was untouched, and the machinery necessary to do the work had to be disassembled, brought inside, and reassembled to do the job.

The White House has been the setting for numerous events of Earth-shattering importance, but it has also hosted an interesting collection of very happy events. To date, 17 White House weddings have been documented. The first was in 1812, in the building's original configuration; the most recent, in 1994.

MARCH 29, 1812:
Lucy Payne Washington (1777–1846) married Thomas Todd (1765–1826) on the State Floor, probably in the Blue Room. Lucy was First Lady Dolley Madison's younger sister. It was the second marriage for both of them, and they had three children together.

Lucy's first husband, planter and militia officer George Steptoe Washington (1771–1809), was George Washington's nephew. They married in 1793, when she was 15, which estranged her from her family for a time. They eventually reconciled, and Lucy and George had four children.

Thomas married Elizabeth Harris in 1788 and had five children with her. He was a lawyer and a judge.

In 1807, President Thomas Jefferson appointed Thomas to the Supreme Court.

MARCH 9, 1820:

Maria Hester Monroe (1803–50) married Samuel Lawrence Gouverneur (1799–1865) on the State Floor, probably in the Blue Room. Maria was the youngest child of the President and First Lady; Samuel was a nephew of First Lady Elizabeth Monroe. This wedding, the first White House wedding of a President's child, was widely criticized because the Monroes chose to keep it private: the guest list included a scant 42 family members and friends. Samuel and Maria had three children. President John Quincy Adams appointed him Postmaster of New York City in 1828 (he held the post until 1836), and he later worked for the US Department of State (1844–49). After Elizabeth Monroe's death, retired President James lived with Maria and Samuel for the last year of his life. In September 1851, a year after Maria's death, Samuel married Mary Digges Lee (1810–98).

FEBRUARY 25, 1828:

John Adams II (1803–34) married Mary Catherine Hellen (1806–70) in the Blue Room. John was the second son of John Quincy and Louisa Adams (and a grandson of second President John Adams); Mary was a niece of Louisa Adams. Mary lived with the Adamses after the deaths of her parents, and all three Adams boys (John, his older brother, George, and his younger brother, Charles) were rivals for her attentions; neither George nor Charles attended the wedding. They had two daughters, though Mary outlived them both. While John Quincy Adams was President, John II served as his private secretary, but after he left office, John II failed in his attempts at a business career, and he died young. Mary continued to live with the retired Presidential couple and cared for them in their old age.

APRIL 10, 1832:

Mary Ann Eastin (1810–47) married planter Lucius J. Polk (1802–70) in the East Room. Mary was a niece of Emily Donelson, whose father was Rachel Jackson's brother. At the time of the wedding, Emily was the first White House hostess for her widowed uncle, Andrew Jackson, and Mary was her assistant. Lucius served in the Tennessee Senate (1831–33) and as Adjutant General for the State of Tennessee (1851–53). Mary and Lucius had one son.

NOVEMBER 29, 1832:

Mary Anne Lewis (born in 1804) married Alphonse Pageot in the East Room. She was a daughter of Major William Berkeley Lewis, who was a quartermaster under General Andrew Jackson and then appointed Auditor of the Treasury when Jackson was President. Alphonse was a diplomat, Secretary of the French Legation and brother-in-law of the French Minister, and later Ambassador to the US. They had one son.

JANUARY 31, 1842:

Elizabeth Tyler (1823–50) married William Waller in the East Room. Elizabeth was the fifth of the seven children of President John Tyler and his first wife, Letitia. She died at the age of 27 from childbirth complications.

MAY 21, 1874:

Ellen Wrenshall "Nellie" Grant (1855–1922) married Algernon Charles Frederick Sartoris (1851–93) in the East Room. She was the only daughter of Ulysses and Julia Grant; he was a wealthy English singer, the son of opera singer Adelaide Kemble and the nephew of actress Fanny Kemble. They had four children and lived together in England for a time, but later separated. At Algernon's death, Nellie was left a wealthy young widow.

She later married Frank Hatch Jones (1854–1931), a lawyer who was Chairman of the Sangamon County Democratic Committee, President of the State League of Democratic Clubs of Illinois, and Secretary of the Illinois State Bar Association.

At the time of her father's death, she was honored with a popular poem, "Nellie," by writer Eugene Field.

JUNE 1878:

Emily Platt (1850–1919) married Russell Hastings (1835–1904) in the Blue Room. Emily was the niece of Lucy Hayes; Russell served on General Rutherford Hayes's staff during the Civil War before being promoted to Brigadier General himself.

JUNE 2, 1886:

President Grover Cleveland (1837–1908) married Frances Folsom (1864–1947) in the Blue Room. Grover was the only President to marry in the White House; Frances was the daughter of his law partner, Oscar Folsom, and then Grover's ward after Oscar's death. The evening ceremony came after a usual working day for the President. It was a small affair, attended by relatives, close friends, members of the Cabinet, and their wives. John Philip Sousa and the Marine Band provided the music. The couple spent a five-day honeymoon at Deer Park in the Cumberland Mountains of Western Maryland. They had five children, the second of whom, Esther, was the only child of a President to be born in the White House, on September 9, 1893.

The Clevelands' marriage license, on display at the Grover Cleveland Birthplace in Caldwell, New Jersey, is fascinating in that all the witnesses were members of the President's Cabinet. Also on display is the silver dollar Cleveland paid for the license, upon which the clerk etched on the edge a note that it was from the President for his marriage license.

Following Grover's death in 1908, Frances married Thomas J. Preston (1863–1955)—a professor of archeology at Princeton University—in 1913. She was the first Presidential widow to remarry. Following her death, on October 29, 1947, she was buried next to Grover in Princeton.

FEBRUARY 17, 1906:

Alice Lee Roosevelt (1884–1980) married Nicholas Longworth III (1869–1931) in the East Room. Alice was the daughter of President Theodore Roosevelt and his deceased first wife, Alice Hathaway Lee; Nicholas was a member of the House of Representatives, representing Ohio. He would go on to be the 43rd Speaker of the House (1925–31). Nicholas and Alice had a daughter, Paulina Longworth, in 1925, though it was generally accepted knowledge in Washington that the girl was actually the daughter of Idaho Senator William Borah (1865–1940). Paulina died of suicide in 1957. Alice remained in Washington following her husband's death and maintained her place in the Washington social and political scenes. In his statement marking her death, President Jimmy Carter wrote, "She had style, she had grace, and she had a sense of humor that kept generations of political newcomers to Washington wondering which was worse—to be skewered by her wit or to be ignored by her."

NOVEMBER 25, 1913:

Jessie Woodrow Wilson (1887–1933) married Francis Bowes Sayre (1885–1972) in the East Room. Jessie was the second daughter of President Woodrow Wilson and his first wife, Ellen, and a college graduate; Francis was a graduate of Harvard Law School and a district attorney. They had three children, the first of whom, Francis B. Sayre, Jr. (1915–2008), was born in the White House; he was Dean of the National Cathedral in Washington, DC (1951–78). While they were living in Massachusetts, Jessie worked for the Democratic Party and the League of Women Voters, and served on the national board of the YWCA. In 1928, she made the introductory speech for Presidential nominee Al Smith at the Democratic National Convention. She died following abdominal surgery. Francis, Sr., was a law professor and college administrator, and also served as a foreign-affairs advisor to the government of King Chulalongkorn of Siam. He was later Assistant Secretary of State, High Commissioner of the Philippines, and US Representative to the United Nations Trusteeship Council.

MAY 7, 1914:

Eleanor Randolph Wilson (1889–1967) married William Gibbs McAdoo (1863–1941) in the Blue Room. Eleanor was the youngest daughter of President Woodrow Wilson and his first wife, Ellen; William was at the time the 46th Secretary of the Treasury. Eleanor and William had two daughters, and after he left the Cabinet, he worked as a lawyer in Washington. They then moved to California, where he made unsuccessful runs for the Democratic nomination for President in 1920 and 1924 (he served in the Senate from 1933 to 1938). Eleanor and William divorced in 1934. In 1937, Eleanor wrote a biography of her father, *The Woodrow Wilsons*.

AUGUST 7, 1918:

Alice Wilson (1895–1970) married Isaac Stuart McElroy, Jr. (1892–1983), in the Blue Room. Alice's father was President Woodrow Wilson's brother;

Isaac was a Presbyterian minister. It was the third White House wedding of Wilson's term (not counting his own second marriage, which took place off the White House grounds, at his new bride's home).

JULY 30, 1942:

Harry Lloyd Hopkins (1890–1946) married Louise Gill Macy (1906–63) in the Second Floor Oval Room, which was the President's study; it was Harry's third marriage and Louise's second. Harry was one of President Franklin Roosevelt's closest advisors (he'd been the eighth Secretary of Commerce (1938–40)); Louise was a former editor for *Harper's Bazaar*.

Harry had first married Ethel Gross in 1913, and they had three sons, before divorcing in 1930. In 1931, he married Barbara Duncan, with whom he had one daughter, before Barbara died of cancer in 1937. On May 10, 1940, after a long night of discussing the German invasion of the Netherlands, Belgium, and Luxembourg, Roosevelt urged Harry to stay for dinner and then the night, in a second-floor White House bedroom. Hopkins wound up sleeping in that bedroom for the next three and a half years. Even after his marriage, Roosevelt asked the couple to stay. They only moved out on December 21, 1943, when Louise demanded a home of their own, and they moved into a Georgetown townhouse.

DECEMBER 9, 1967:

Lynda Bird Johnson (born March 19, 1944) married Charles Spittal "Chuck" Robb (born June 26, 1939) in the East Room. Lynda is the elder daughter of President Lyndon Baines and Lady Bird Johnson; Chuck, a member of the US Marine Corps, was at the time a White House social aide. After the wedding, Chuck served a tour of duty in Vietnam, winning the Bronze Star. After the war, he earned a JD, practiced law, served as Lieutenant Governor and Governor of Virginia (1978–82 and 1982–86), and then as a Senator (1989–2001). Later in life, he taught and served on several government commissions. Lynda served as Chairman of the Board of Reading is Fundamental and was a contributing editor to *Ladies Home Journal* magazine. She also serves on the Board of Directors of the Lyndon Baines Johnson Foundation and the Lady Bird Johnson

Wildflower Center. Lynda and Chuck have three daughters and several grandchildren.

JUNE 12, 1971:

Patricia "Tricia" Nixon (born February 21, 1946) married Edward Finch Cox (born October 2, 1946) in the Rose Garden. Tricia is the elder daughter of President Richard and Pat Nixon; Edward is a lawyer and has held many appointed governmental positions at the state and federal levels. Tricia serves on the boards of directors of several medical research institutions and on the board of the Richard Nixon Foundation at the Nixon Library in California. Edward became Chairman of the New York State Republican Committee in 2008. Tricia and Edward have one son, Christopher, who is also a lawyer.

MAY 28, 1994:

Anthony Dean "Tony" Rodham (born in 1954) married Nicole Boxer (born in 1967) in the Rose Garden. Tony is the youngest brother of First Lady Hillary Rodham Clinton; Nicole is the daughter of California Senator Barbara Boxer. They had a son, Zachary, in 1995, before separating in 2000 and then eventually divorcing. For a time, Zachary had the unique distinction of being simultaneously the grandson and nephew of sitting US Senators. Tony is a business consultant and fund-raiser. In 2005, he married Megan Madden, with whom he has two children. Nicole is a documentary film producer; she married Kevin E. Keegan, Jr., with whom she has one child.

54. Non-White House Weddings of Presidential Children

In addition to the nine Presidential children who chose to marry in the White House during their fathers' terms of office, another 12 married while their fathers were President, but did so somewhere else.

ANDREW JACKSON, JR. (1808–65), the adopted son of Andrew and Rachel Jackson (he was the son of Rachel's brother, Severn Donelson), married Sarah Yorke (1803–87) in Philadelphia, Pennsylvania, on November 24, 1831. After an extended honeymoon at the White House, they returned to Jackson's Tennessee plantation, The Hermitage, which they managed until a fire destroyed much of the main house in 1834. They and their two young children (they would eventually have five, though only three lived to adulthood) then moved into the White House, arriving on November 26, 1834. Sarah served as the widowed President's White House hostess, at first in concert with his niece, Emily Donelson, and then alone after Emily's death in 1836.

ABRAHAM VAN BUREN (1807–73)—the eldest of the four children of Martin and Hannah Van Buren—married Angelica Singleton (1818–77) on November 27, 1838, at her family's Home Place Plantation in South Carolina (President Van Buren was unable to attend). Abraham graduated from West Point in 1827 and rose to the rank of Captain before resigning his commission the day before his father's inauguration, in order to become the President's private secretary. In 1838, former First Lady Dolley Madison introduced Abraham to her cousin, Angelica, at a White House dinner. They fell in love and married later in the year. Following their wedding, Angelica took over the duties of White House hostess for her widowed father-in-law. In 1846, Abraham rejoined the Army with the rank of Major; in 1847, he was made a brevet Lieutenant

Colonel. He served as an aide to Generals Zachary Taylor and Winfield Scott. In 1848, Abraham and Angelica moved to New York City, and in 1854, he retired from the Army. Abraham and Angelica had four children.

FREDERICK DENT GRANT (1850–1912)—the first of the four children of Ulysses and Julia Grant—married Ida Marie Honoré (1854–1930) on October 20, 1874, at the Honoré home in Louisville, Kentucky, with the President and Mrs. Grant in attendance. Frederick had graduated from West Point in 1871 and met Ida on one of his leaves; she was studying music in Washington. Following the wedding and honeymoon, Ida lived in the White House with her in-laws while Frederick returned to the Army, where he took part in General George Custer's Black Hills expedition of 1875. He was given leave to return home for the birth of his first child, Julia Dent Grant, so he was not with Custer at the Battle of the Little Big Horn. Frederick retired from the Army in 1881—the year his son, Ulysses III, was born—to help his father prepare his memoirs. In 1889, Benjamin Harrison appointed Frederick Minister to Austria-Hungary, and he stayed on under Grover Cleveland, resigning in 1893. He was Commissioner of the New York City Police Department from 1894 to 1898 (his term overlapped Theodore Roosevelt's time as Superintendent of the same force). At the outbreak of the Spanish-American War in 1898, Frederick rejoined the Army, and at the time of his death, he was Commander of the Eastern Division, with the rank of Major General. Ida moved to Florida and, later in life, to Washington. Frederick and Ida are buried in West Point Cemetery.

ELLIOTT ROOSEVELT (1910–90)—the third child of Franklin and Eleanor Roosevelt—had a widely varied career, including stints in broadcasting, ranching, politics, and business. He was perhaps most successful in his military career: he was commissioned a Captain in the US Army Air Corps on his 30th birthday, in 1940. During World War II, he rose to the rank of Brigadier General, commanding several reconnaissance units. He left the Army in 1945.

Elliott married for the first time in 1932. He and his wife had one son before they divorced on July 17, 1933.

On July 22, 1933, he married Texas heiress Ruth Josephine Googins (1908–74) in Burlintgon, Iowa, on her aunt and uncle's estate. His parents were unable to attend, but his sister Anna did. Elliott and Ruth had three children before divorcing in March 1944. Ruth remarried that June.

Elliot next married actress Faye Margaret Emerson (1917–83) on December 3, 1944 (it was her second of three marriages). They were introduced by Howard Hughes, and their wedding took place on an observation platform overlooking the Grand Canyon. They divorced in 1950. Faye was later nominated for two Emmy Awards and has two stars on the Hollywood Walk of Fame (one for television, one for movies). She spent her final years living in Spain, with John Aspinwall Roosevelt's divorced first wife.

Elliot married two further times.

Anna Eleanor Roosevelt, Jr. (1906–75)—the oldest of Franklin and Eleanor Roosevelt's children—was a writer and editor, involved in managing or owning several newspapers. Later in life, she was a public-relations executive. She also lived in the White House for a time, assisting her parents, and traveled with her father to the Yalta Conference (her brother Elliott had accompanied him to earlier meetings, but had become a political liability).

Anna married for the first time in 1926. She had two children before divorcing in July 1934.

On January 18, 1935, she married journalist Clarence John Boettiger (1900–50) in the Roosevelts' New York City home. It was his second marriage as well. Clarence was hired to be the publisher of the *Seattle Post-Intelligencer*, and Anna served as editor of the women's page. When Clarence joined the military in 1943, Anna left the paper as well. She moved into the White House in 1944. Following FDR's death, Anna and Clarence bought and ran the weekly *Arizona Times*. They sold the paper in 1948 and divorced in 1949. He remarried later that year and committed suicide in 1950.

Anna married for a third time in 1952. In 1963, President Kennedy appointed Anna to the Citizen's Advisory Council on the Status of Women, and in 1968, she was appointed Vice-Chairman of the President's Commission for the Observance of Human Rights.

FRANKLIN DELANO ROOSEVELT, JR. (1914–88)—the fifth of Franklin and Eleanor Roosevelt's six children—graduated from law school in June 1940 and then joined the Naval Reserve. During World War II, he rose to the rank of Lieutenant Commander and commanded the destroyer escort USS *Ulvert M. Moore* (DE-442), which was in Tokyo Bay when Japan formally surrendered on September 2, 1945. He earned the Silver Star, Bronze Star, Purple Heart, and 12 battle stars. After the war, he worked as a lawyer, and served in the House of Representatives, representing New York, from 1949 to 1955. He was Under Secretary of Commerce from 1963 to 1965, and President Johnson appointed him the first Chairman of the Equal Employment Opportunity Commission.

Franklin Jr. married for the first time on June 30, 1937, when he married heiress Ethel Du Pont (1916–65). The ceremony was held at Christ Church, Christiana Hundred, Delaware, with a reception following at the bride's parents' estate, Owl's Nest. The couple was featured on the cover of *Time* magazine. They had two sons before divorcing in 1949. Ethel remarried in 1950 and committed suicide in 1965.

Franklin Jr. married four more times and had three more children.

JOHN ASPINWALL ROOSEVELT II (1916–81)—the youngest of Franklin and Eleanor Roosevelt's children—served in the Navy during World War II, rising to the rank of Lieutenant Commander but never commanding a unit. After the war, he worked in business and finance, and served on the boards of many organizations, including the Greater New York Council of Boy Scouts of America, Roosevelt University, and the State University of New York. Alone of the Roosevelt sons, he never sought political office.

John married for the first time on June 18, 1938, in Nahant, Massachusetts. His bride was Boston socialite Anne Lindsay Clark

(1916–73), and his parents traveled by special train to attend the wedding. They had four children and divorced in 1965. After their marriage ended, Anne moved to Mallorca, Spain, where she lived with Elliott Roosevelt's divorced third wife, Faye Emerson.

On October 28, 1965, he married Irene Boyd McAlpin (born in 1931).

JAMES ROOSEVELT II (1907–91)—the second of Franklin and Eleanor Roosevelt's children—was a law-school student and at the same time an insurance salesman; he was so successful at the latter that he dropped out of law school and soon founded his own insurance company. He left in 1937 when he was appointed Secretary to the President. He worked in the White House for just over a year and then moved to California. During World War II, he served in the US Marine Corps and rose to the rank of Brigadier General, winning the Navy Cross and the Silver Star. After the war, he returned to his insurance company. He represented California in the House of Representatives from 1955 to 1965, when President Johnson appointed him a delegate to the United Nations Educational, Scientific, and Cultural Organization (UNESCO).

James married for the first time in 1930, having two children and then divorcing in 1940.

On April 14, 1941, he married Romelle Theresa Schneider (1915–2002), a nurse, in Beverly Hills, California. They had three children and divorced in 1955.

He married two more times.

LUCI BAINES JOHNSON (born July 2, 1947) married Air National Guardsman Patrick Nugent (born July 8, 1943) on August 6, 1966, at the Shrine of the Immaculate Conception in Washington. After the ceremony, the President and Mrs. Johnson hosted a reception for about 700 guests in the White House. (When Luci's older sister, Lynda, married the following year, the ceremony was in the White House.) The wedding was broadcast on television (drawing 55 million viewers) and was featured on the cover of *Life* magazine's August 19, 1966, issue. Luci and Patrick had four children and divorced in 1979.

On March 3, 1984, she married Ian J. Turpin (born in 1944), a Scottish-born Canadian financier; he is now President of LBJ Asset Management Partners at LBJ Ranch.

MAUREEN REAGAN (1941–2001)—the first child of President Ronald Reagan and his first wife, Jane Wyman—was an actor, political activist, and the first daughter of a President to run for political office (she lost elections for the Senate (1982) and the House of Representatives (1992) in California).

Maureen married for the first time in 1961. Her husband, John Filippone, was a policeman. They divorced in 1962.

On February 28, 1964, she married David G. Sills (1938–2011), a lawyer and Marine Corps officer. They divorced in 1967.

On April 25, 1981, she married Dennis Revell at the Beverly Hills Hotel. Dennis is the CEO of Revell Communications and active in Republican politics in California. Maureen and Dennis adopted a Ugandan-born daughter in 1994.

PATRICIA ANN "PATTI" DAVIS (born October 21, 1952)—the first child of President Ronald Reagan and his second wife, Nancy Davis—is an actress and author. On August 14, 1984, she married yoga instructor Paul Grilley at the Bel-Air Hotel in Los Angeles, California, with her parents in attendance. Patti and Paul divorced in 1990.

DOROTHY WALKER "DORO" BUSH (born August 18, 1959)—the youngest child of George H.W. and Barbara Bush—is a fund-raiser and author. She wrote the book *My Father, My President: A Personal Account of the Life of George H.W. Bush*. She is the co-chair of the Barbara Bush Foundation for Family Literacy and, in 2009, was the sponsor of the aircraft carrier USS *George H.W. Bush* (CVN-77).

Doro married for the first time in 1982, when her father was Vice President. She married William Heekin LeBlond (born January 11, 1957). They had two children and divorced in 1990.

On June 26, 1992, Doro married Washington lobbyist Robert Koch (born in 1960) at Camp David. She is the only Presidential child to be married at Camp David. Doro and Robert have two children.

JENNA WELCH BUSH (born November 25, 1981)—the younger fraternal-twin daughter of George W. and Laura Bush—is an author, an editor-at-large for *Southern Living* magazine, a special correspondent for NBC's *Today Show*, and a contributor to *NBC Nightly News*. On May 10, 2008, she married investment banker Henry Chase Hager (born May 9, 1978) at her parents' Prairie Chapel Ranch near Crawford, Texas. The President and Mrs. Bush hosted a reception for the newlyweds at the White House on June 21, 2008. Jenna and Henry have two daughters.

55. The Roosevelts: the Most-Married Presidential Children

The average President was married 1.15 times. The average First Lady was married 1.3 times. The average Roosevelt child was married 3.8 times.

Franklin and Eleanor Roosevelt had six children, five of whom lived to adulthood:

1. ANNA ELEANOR ROOSEVELT (May 3, 1906–December 1, 1975)—married three times, had three children
2. JAMES ROOSEVELT II (December 23, 1907–August 13, 1991)—married four times, had seven children
3. FRANKLIN ROOSEVELT (March 18–November 1, 1909)
4. ELLIOTT ROOSEVELT (September 23, 1910–October 27, 1990)—married five times, had five children
5. FRANKLIN DELANO ROOSEVELT, JR. (August 17, 1914–August 17, 1988)—married five times, had five children
6. JOHN ASPINWALL ROOSEVELT II (March 13, 1916–April 27, 1981)—married two times, had four children

ANNA ELEANOR ROOSEVELT, JR., was a writer and editor involved in managing or owning several newspapers. Later in life, she was a public relations executive. She also lived in the White House for a time, assisting her parents, and traveled with her father to the Yalta Conference (her brother Elliott had accompanied him to earlier meetings, but had become a political liability).

Anna married for the first time in 1926. Her husband was stockbroker Curtis Bean Dall (1896–1991). They had two children, but by the time FDR was elected President, Anna and Curtis's marriage wasn't working, and she lived in the White House with her parents. Anna and Curtis divorced in July 1934.

On January 18, 1935, she married journalist Clarence John Boettiger (1900–50) in the Roosevelts' New York City home. It was his second marriage as well. Clarence was the publisher of the *Seattle Post-Intelligencer*, and Anna edited the women's page. When Clarence joined the military in 1943, Anna left the paper. She moved into the White House in 1944. After her father's death, Anna and Clarence bought the weekly *Arizona Times*, but they sold the paper in 1948 and divorced in 1949. He remarried later that year and committed suicide in 1950.

In 1952, Anna married Dr. James Addison Halsted (1905–84) and started working in public relations. In 1958, Anna and James moved to Iran, where he helped establish the Pahlavi University Medical School. In 1960, they moved back to Kentucky, and Anna worked at the University of Kentucky Medical Center. In 1961, they moved to Michigan, where Anna worked at the Metropolitan Hospital and then the Wayne State University School of Medicine.

In 1963, President Kennedy appointed Anna to the Citizen's Advisory Council on the Status of Women, and Anna and James moved to Washington in 1964. In 1968, she was appointed Vice-Chairman of the President's Commission for the Observance of Human Rights.

JAMES ROOSEVELT II was a student at the Boston University School of Law and at the same time an insurance salesman; he was so successful in insurance that he dropped out of law school, and, in 1932, founded his own insurance company. He left in 1937 when he was appointed Secretary to the President. He worked in the White House for just over a year and then moved to California. During World War II, he served in the US Marine Corps and rose to the rank of Brigadier General, winning the Navy Cross and the Silver Star. After the war, he returned to his insurance company. He represented California in the House of Representatives from 1955 to 1965, when President Johnson appointed him a delegate to the United Nations Educational, Scientific, and Cultural Organization (UNESCO).

James married for the first time in 1930. His wife was socialite Betsey Maria Cushing (1908–98); she and her two sisters were known in the social world as the "Cushing Sisters." Their mother urged them to pursue husbands of wealth and prominence. Betsey's older sister, Mary, married Vincent Astor, and her younger sister, Barbara, married Standard Oil heir Stanley Mortimer, Jr., and CBS founder William S. Paley. James and Betsey had two daughters and divorced in 1940. (Betsey later married millionaire John Hay Whitney, whom President Eisenhower appointed Ambassador to the UK.)

On April 14, 1941, James married Romelle Theresa Schneider (1915–2002), a nurse, in Beverly Hills, California. They had three children and divorced in 1955.

On July 2, 1956, he married his receptionist, Gladys Irene Owens (1917–87). They had one son and divorced in 1969.

On October 3, 1969, he married Mary Lena Winskill (born in 1939), who was his youngest son's teacher. They had one daughter, Rebecca, in 1971.

James had seven children. His oldest daughter, Sara, was 39 years older than his youngest, Rebecca. Sara had five children before Rebecca was born.

ELLIOTT ROOSEVELT had a widely varied career, including stints in broadcasting, ranching, politics, and business. He was perhaps most successful in his military career: he was commissioned a Captain in the US Army Air Corps on his 30th birthday, in 1940. During World War II, he rose to the rank of Brigadier General, commanding several reconnaissance units and accompanying his father to several conferences. He left the Army in 1945.

Elliott married for the first time on January 16, 1932. His wife was Elizabeth Browning Donner (1911–80). They had one son before divorcing in 1933 (their divorce was finalized on July 17).

On July 22, 1933, he married Texas heiress Ruth Josephine Googins (1908–74) in Burlington, Iowa, on her aunt and uncle's estate. His parents were unable to attend, but his sister Anna did. Elliott and Ruth had three children before divorcing in March 1944. Ruth remarried that June.

Elliot next married actress Faye Margaret Emerson (1917–83) on December 3, 1944 (it was her second of three marriages). They were introduced by Howard Hughes, and their wedding took place on an observation platform overlooking the Grand Canyon. They divorced in 1950. Faye was later nominated for two Emmy Awards and has two stars on the Hollywood Walk of Fame (one for television, one for movies). She spent her final years living in Spain, with John Aspinwall Roosevelt's divorced first wife.

Fourteen months after his third divorce, Elliott married Minnewa Bell (1911–83), on March 15, 1951. They divorced in 1960

On November 3, 1960, Elliott married Patricia Peabody Whitehead (1922–96). Her four children from a previous marriage adopted the Roosevelt surname. Elliot and Patricia's one child together died as an infant.

FRANKLIN DELANO ROOSEVELT, JR., graduated from law school in June 1940 and then joined the Naval Reserve. During World War II, he rose to the rank of Lieutenant Commander, and commanded the destroyer escort USS *Ulvert M. Moore* (DE-442), which was in Tokyo Bay when Japan formally surrendered on September 2, 1945. He earned the Silver Star, Bronze Star, Purple Heart, and 12 battle stars. After the war, he worked as a lawyer and served in the House of Representatives, representing New York, from 1949 to 1955. He was Under Secretary of Commerce from 1963 to 1965, and President Johnson appointed him the first Chairman of the Equal Employment Opportunity Commission.

Franklin married for the first time on June 30, 1937, when he married heiress Ethel Du Pont (1916–65). The ceremony was held at Christ Church, Christiana Hundred, Delaware, with a reception following at the bride's parents' estate, Owl's Nest. The couple was featured on the cover of *Time* magazine. They had two sons before divorcing in 1949. Ethel remarried in 1950 and committed suicide in 1965.

On August 31, 1949, he married Suzanne Perrin (1921–?). They had two daughters and divorced in 1970.

On July 1, 1970, he married Felicia Schiff Warburg Sarnoff (1927–?). It was her third marriage as well. They divorced in 1976.

On May 6, 1977, he married Patricia Luisa Oakes (born in 1951). They had one son before divorcing in 1981.

On March 3, 1984, he married Linda McKay Stevenson Weicker (born in 1939). They were married until his death.

JOHN ASPINWALL ROOSEVELT II served in the Navy during World War II, rising to the rank of Lieutenant Commander, but never commanding a unit. After the war, he worked in business and finance, and served on the boards of many organizations, including the Greater New York Council of Boy Scouts of America, Roosevelt University, and the State University of New York. Alone of the Roosevelt sons, he never sought political office.

John married for the first time on June 18, 1938, in Nahant, Massachusetts. His bride was Boston socialite Anne Lindsay Clark (1916–73), and his parents traveled by special train to attend the wedding. They had four children and divorced in 1965. After their marriage ended, Anne moved to Mallorca, Spain, where she lived with Elliott Roosevelt's divorced third wife, Faye Emerson.

On October 28, 1965, he married Irene Boyd McAlpin (born in 1931), who was with him until his death.

56. Presidential Pets

While Washington is frequently referred to as a political zoo, the White House has at times more closely resembled an actual zoo. And while there is no definitive list of all the animals who've lived there as pets (let alone animals kept there for labor, food, or other reasons), anecdotal evidence shows some of the love Presidents and their families have had for non-human creatures.

Far and away, the most popular type of animal companion kept by Presidents has been dogs, but there have also been many cats, horses, and birds. Some of the less common pet types have included John Quincy Adams's silk worms, Martin Van Buren's tiger cubs (a gift from the Sultan of Oman), Benjamin Harrison's opossums (known as Mr. Reciprocity and Mr. Protection), Theodore Roosevelt's hyena, and Calvin Coolidge's pygmy hippopotamus, wallaby, and duiker.

The only two Presidents with no known pets were Chester Arthur (1881–85) and Andrew Johnson (1865–69), though Johnson did feed the white mice he found in his bedroom.

In October 1863, Abraham Lincoln (1861–65) issued a proclamation marking the last Thursday of November as Thanksgiving Day. After the proclamation, a turkey was sent to the White House for Thanksgiving dinner, but Lincoln's son Tad made a pet of the bird, named him Tom, and begged for a stay of execution. Lincoln issued an order of reprieve, sparing the turkey's life and inaugurating the Presidential custom of pardoning a turkey on Thanksgiving.

In 1878, President Rutherford Hayes received the first documented Siamese cats to reach the United States. Named Siam and Miss Pussy, they were gifts from the King of Siam via the American Consul in Bangkok.

William McKinley (1897–1901) was the last President to not have a dog in the White House.

William Howard Taft's (1909–13) Holstein cow, Pauline Wayne, was the last cow to live at the White House. The cow was a gift from Wisconsin Senator Isaac Stephenson. Kept for her milk, the cow was considered both a pet and livestock.

Calvin Coolidge's (1923–29) personal menagerie was one of the greatest in the White House. It included dogs, cats, a bobcat, a goose, a donkey, lion cubs, an antelope, and a wallaby. But the main attraction was probably Billy, a pygmy hippopotamus born in Liberia that was given to the President by tire mogul Harvey Firestone in 1927. In his 1929 autobiography, Coolidge wrote about his collection and said he'd donated many of the animals, including Billy, to the Smithsonian National Zoological Park. Coolidge's was the second largest collection of Presidential animals donated to the National Zoo (after Theodore Roosevelt's). Billy—later known as William Johnson Hippopotamus—was the eighth pygmy hippopotamus brought to the United States. He lived until 1955 and is the common ancestor to most pygmy hippos in US zoos; he sired 23 calves.

George H.W. and Barbara Bush's (1989–93) English Springer Spaniel Millie (1985–97) is credited as the author of *Millie's Book: As Dictated to Barbara Bush*, which reached #1 on the *New York Times* bestseller nonfiction list. In 1989, Millie gave birth to a litter of six puppies, including Spot Fetcher (1989–2004), who became the only second-generation White House dog with George W. Bush (2001–09).

Presidential families and their known types of pets:

GEORGE WASHINGTON: Dog, horse, donkey.
JOHN ADAMS: Dog, horse.
THOMAS JEFFERSON: Dog, bird, horse, bear cub.
JAMES MADISON: Bird.
JAMES MONROE: Dog.
JOHN QUINCY ADAMS: Silk worms.
ANDREW JACKSON: Horse, bird.
MARTIN VAN BUREN: Tiger cub.
WILLIAM HARRISON: Cow, goat.
JOHN TYLER: Dog, horse, bird.

JAMES POLK: Horse.

ZACHARY TAYLOR: Horse.

MILLARD FILLMORE: Horse.

FRANKLIN PIERCE: Dog, bird.

JAMES BUCHANAN: Dog, bird.

ABRAHAM LINCOLN: Dog, cat, horse, goat, rabbit, turkey.

ANDREW JOHNSON: Fed the mice in his bedroom.

ULYSSES GRANT: Dog, horse.

RUTHERFORD HAYES: Dog, cat.

JAMES GARFIELD: Dog, horse.

CHESTER ARTHUR: None known.

GROVER CLEVELAND: Dog, bird.

BENJAMIN HARRISON: Dog, goat, opossum.

WILLIAM MCKINLEY: Cat, bird.

THEODORE ROOSEVELT: Dog, cat, horse, bird, bear, badger, guinea pig, hyena, pig, rabbit, rat, snake.

WILLIAM TAFT: Dog, cow.

WOODROW WILSON: Dog, cat, bird, sheep.

WARREN HARDING: Dog, squirrel.

CALVIN COOLIDGE: Dog, cat, donkey, bird, bear, bobcat, duiker, raccoon, lion cub, pygmy hippopotamus, wallaby.

HERBERT HOOVER: Dog, alligator.

FRANKLIN ROOSEVELT: Dog.

HARRY TRUMAN: Dog.

DWIGHT EISENHOWER: Dog.

JOHN KENNEDY: Dog, cat, horse, bird, hamster, rabbit.

LYNDON JOHNSON: Dog, bird, hamster.

RICHARD NIXON: Dog.

GERALD FORD: Dog, cat.

JIMMY CARTER: Dog, cat.

RONALD REAGAN: Dog, horse (these horses did not live at the White House).

GEORGE H.W. BUSH: Dog.

BILL CLINTON: Dog, cat.

GEORGE W. BUSH: Dog, cat, cow (this cow did not live at the White House).

BARACK OBAMA: Dog.

SUMMATIONS

57. The Most Common First Ladies (Those Appearing in the Fewest Lists in this Book)

Considering ranked lists, four are tied with no appearances whatsoever:

1 (tie). LOUISA ADAMS (1825–29)
1 (tie). MARY LINCOLN (1861–65)
1 (tie). ELIZA JOHNSON (1865–69)
1 (tie). HELEN TAFT (1909–13)

Ten more appear on one list each. Ranked by their ranking on those lists, we have:

5. MICHELLE OBAMA (2009–): The First Ladies with the Most Living Predecessors (she's in a seven-way tie for fifth place).

6. PAT NIXON: (1969–74): The Five Longest Presidential Marriages (fifth place).

7 (tie). JANE WYMAN REAGAN: The Five Briefest Presidential Marriages (fourth place).

7 (tie). JANE PIERCE (1853–57): The Five First Ladies Who Died the Youngest (fourth place).

7 (tie). ELLEN ARTHUR: The Five First Ladies Who Died the Youngest (fourth place among those who died before their President-husbands' terms of office).

10 (tie). JULIA GRANT (1869–77): The First Ladies Who Served the Longest Terms (she's in a seven-way tie for second place).

10 (tie). MAMIE EISENHOWER (1953–61): The First Ladies Who Served the Longest Terms (she's in a seven-way tie for second place). Her husband, Dwight, is the second most common President, appearing on only one ranked list in *The Presidential Book of Lists*.

10 (tie). ABIGAIL ADAMS (1797–1801): The First Ladies with the Fewest Living Predecessors (second place).

13. CAROLINE FILLMORE: The First Ladies Who Had the Fewest Children (she's in a four-way tie for first place).

58. The Most Uncommon First Ladies (Those Appearing in the Most Lists in this Book)

1. FRANCES CLEVELAND (1886–89 and 1893–97) appears on five ranked lists, but owing to her husband's non-consecutive terms of office, she makes two appearances on two of the lists: The First Ladies Who Lived the Longest after Leaving the White House (#1); The First Ladies Who Outlived the Greatest Number of Their Successors (#3); The Five First Ladies Who Outlived Their Husbands by the Longest Time (#3); The Five Youngest First Ladies (#1 and #3 (first when she married President Cleveland, and third when they returned to the White House after Benjamin Harrison's term)); The First Ladies Who Were the Greatest Number of Years Younger Than Their Predecessors (she appears twice on this list, at #2 and at #4).

Two First Ladies appear on six ranked lists each, but ranking them based on their positions on the lists yields:

2. JULIA TYLER (1844–45) appears on six ranked lists: The First Ladies Who Lived the Longest after Leaving the White House (#2); The First Ladies Who Outlived the Greatest Number of Their Successors (tied for #1); The First Ladies Who Had the Most Children (tied for #4); The Five Youngest First Ladies (#2); The First Ladies Who Were the Greatest Number of Years Younger Than Their Predecessors (#3); and The First Ladies Who Served the Shortest Terms (#3).

3. MARY HARRISON (married Benjamin Harrison (1889–93) after he retired from the Presidency) appears on six ranked lists: The Five First Ladies Who Lived the Longest (#6); The First Ladies Who Outlived the

Greatest Number of Their Successors (#4); The First Ladies Who Had the Fewest Children (tied for #5); The First Ladies Who Outlived Their Husbands by the Longest Time (#1); The Five Briefest Presidential Marriages (#2); and The First Ladies Who Were the Greatest Number of Years Younger Than Their Predecessors (#5).

Three First Ladies appear on five ranked lists each, but ranking them based on their positions on the lists yields:

4. SARAH POLK (1845–49) appears on five ranked lists: The First Ladies Who Lived the Longest after Leaving the White House (#3); The First Ladies Who Outlived the Greatest Number of Their Successors (tied for #1); The First Ladies Who Had the Fewest Children (tied for #1); The First Ladies Who Outlived Their Husbands by the Longest Time (#2); and The First Ladies Who Were the Greatest Number of Years Older Than Their Predecessors (#3).

5. BESS TRUMAN (1945–53) appears on five ranked lists: The Five First Ladies Who Lived the Longest (#1); The First Ladies with the Most Living Predecessors (tied for #5); The First Ladies Who Had the Fewest Children (tied for #5); The Five Longest Presidential Marriages (#5); and The Five Oldest First Ladies (#5 or #1, depending on how the age is determined).

6. DOLLEY MADISON (1809–17) appears on five ranked lists: The First Ladies with the Fewest Living Predecessors (#3); The First Ladies Who Had the Fewest Children (tied for #3); The Five Youngest First Ladies (#6); The First Ladies Who Were the Greatest Number of Years Younger Than Their Predecessors (#7); and The First Ladies Who Served the Longest Terms (tied for #2).

INDEX

of people appearing in this book (by chapter/list number, not by page). Bold-faced numbers indicate lists in which the person appears. Numbers not in bold face are supporting characters.